D1361236

© 2006 by Collins

This 2008 edition published by Metro Books,
by arrangement with Collins.

All rights reserved. No part of this publication may be reproduced,
stored in a retrieval system, or transmitted, in any form or by any means,
electronic, mechanical, photocopying, recording, or otherwise,
without prior written permission from the publisher.

Text © Felicity Barnum-Bobb, 2006
Photography © Steve Baxter and Marie-Louise Avery, 2006

Metro Books
122 Fifth Avenue
New York, NY 10011

ISBN-13: 978-1-4351-0944-5
ISBN-10: 1-4351-0944-9

Printed and bound in Hong Kong

10 9 8 7 6 5 4 3 2 1

100 Magnificent Muffins & Scones

Felicity Barnum-Bobb

METRO BOOKS

NEW YORK

Contents

Introduction

What exactly is a muffin? Is it a cake, bun, or type of bread? By working your way through the 100 recipes in this book, you'll discover that it can be all those things. There are muffins and scones here to suit every mood and occasion: whether sweet or savory, healthy or indulgent, for a special diet or a special occasion, mini-muffins for children or batch-baking for a party, this book's got it sorted.

American muffins

This book is bursting with recipes for American muffins. Why? Because they are just so easy to make. They taste fantastic and everyone loves them. And best of all, they take only about 30 minutes. That's the kind of cooking I go for—deeply satisfying yet speedy. Unlike English muffins (see below), these treats contain baking powder, the magic ingredient that makes them rise into divine little cakey treats. Don't get led astray by the store-bought versions, which are always seriously oversweet—real homemade muffins are never too sweet and they can, of course, be savory too.

English muffins

The word "muffin" is thought to have come from an old French word "moufflet," meaning soft and referring to bread. There are references to English muffin recipes as early as 1747, but they were most popular in the nineteenth century.

Making English muffins is quite time-consuming because they use yeast. Although my recipes use active dry yeast to speed things up, you still need to let the dough rise. I don't know about you, but when I'm baking I'm usually looking for instant gratification and I want the process to be fast and easy. My solution is to use a bread maker. Throw all the ingredients in the machine in the order your manufacturer recommends and let it do all the hard work, kneading and proving the dough. Then all you have to do is shape and cook them. Cooking English muffins is different—you don't bake them, they are cooked on a hotplate or a solid flat grill pan, which gives them their traditional flat tops and bottoms. It'll take a few attempts to get them cooked to perfection, but it's worth persevering.

If you have children to entertain (as I regularly do, being a mother of four), I thoroughly recommend making the muffins by hand together. Measuring out the ingredients is a math lesson in itself, and giving each child responsibility for one ingredient will make the whole thing a great team effort. Once the bulk of the dough is made, divide it equally between the children and let them each knead a piece. The great thing about any yeast mixture is that the more you manhandle it, the better the end result will be. Encourage them to vent their anger on the dough, rather than each other; punch it, poke it, and smash it on the table. Even throwing the dough's fine, as long as it's not aimed at someone else!

Scones

These are speedy to make, as they use self-rising flour or baking powder as their raising agent. This Scottish quick bread is said to have taken its name from the Stone of Destiny (or Scone), the place where Scottish kings were once crowned. The original recipe was made with oats and grill-baked. My recipes are more flour-based and are all baked in a hot oven for ease. They come in various shapes, but most commonly as rounds. There is a lot of debate over the pronunciation of the word. It's suggested that if you're posh you say "skown" to rhyme with "cone" while less privileged people say "skon" to rhyme with "gone"! I say that's nonsense, and all that matters is that you enjoy baking and eating them.

Shortcut secrets

You really don't need any fancy equipment to make up these recipes—a large bowl, pitcher, strainer, wooden spoon, and a muffin tray will suffice. However, because I'm usually multi-tasking (feeding the children and baking), I sometimes use a freestanding mixer. They will gently combine the dry ingredients with the wet and won't overmix if used on the lowest setting (which is a good thing, as it can make American-style muffins heavy).

When you need to get your skates on and produce something quickly, get out the food processor and it will charge through the recipe in a matter of minutes—and because you're so short of time you won't overmix. Those are the times when you can forget sifting the flour and it really won't matter—the muffins will taste fine! Use the microwave to melt the butter—30–50 seconds on high (850w) and it's softened enough to use. Use the processor or a coffee grinder to chop nuts speedily.

When the pressure's on, always line the muffin pans with paper liners, as you can always peel them off to serve. There's no need to worry about cooling the muffins on a wire rack—if they're in the paper liners, they're fine to cool in the pans.

That fresh-baked taste

If you're going to the hassle of doing the homemade thing, you'll want everything to taste as good as possible. We're so used to store-bought goods having a long shelf-life that it's easy to forget that these muffins will stay fresh for only a couple of days. The solution? Pop extra muffins into the freezer and reheat in the microwave to serve. One muffin will take 30 seconds on high (850w) to reheat from frozen. Another option is to make up the mixture and leave it in the refrigerator overnight. You could bake half of the muffins on one day and the remainder the next. If you have plenty of space in your freezer and a muffin pan to spare, why not freeze the unbaked muffins in their liners in the pan? Bake from frozen for an extra 5 minutes.

Essential tips for successful baking

- Invest in a set of cook's measuring spoons. Household spoons vary so much in size, so results are not consistent. These recipes were tested with the following measuring spoons:

  5ml = 1tsp, 10ml = 2 tsp, 15ml = 1tbsp.

  All spoon measurements should be level.

- Prepare recipes entirely in metric or imperial—never switch between the two while following a recipe.

- Always set your scales to zero when you measure.

- Check liquid measurements in a pitcher at eye level, or use digital scales which measure liquids too.

- Let melted butter cool for a few minutes before mixing with eggs.

- All eggs are medium unless otherwise stated.

- If using a regular oven, always bake muffins and scones toward the top of the oven.

- To cook in a convection oven, reduce oven temperatures by 20°C (25–35°F), otherwise the muffins will burn (see chart on p.8). Any rack in the oven is suitable since the temperature is even throughout.

- Test readyness by inserting a toothpick into the center of the muffins—it should come out clean.

Baking pan sizes

The muffins in this book come in three different sizes: regular, mini, and king-size.

Although the size of a pan may vary depending on the manufacturer, the following guide will help you to decide on the most appropriate pan for each recipe. Whichever size pan you are using, make sure to divide the mixture evenly between the cups or liners.

Most of the recipes use a regular muffin pan (scant ½ cup/4fl oz/100ml); each cup measures 2in (5cm) at the base, 2¾in (7cm) at the top, and is 1¼in (3cm) deep.

King-size muffins (⅔ cup/5fl oz/150ml) are cooked in pans measuring 2½in (6cm) at the base, 3½in (8½cm) at the top, and 1¾in (4cm) deep.

Mini-muffin pans (2 tbsp/30ml) measure 1¼in (3cm) at the base, 1¾in (4.5cm) at the top, and are ¾in (2cm) deep. Line them with mini-muffin liners (also sold as mini cake liners). When testing the recipes for the children's chapter, I discovered that these mini ones are absolutely teeny, so on occasions I recommend using a regular muffin pan (2fl oz/50ml) with regular liners but only filling each cup halfway.

I suggest you invest in a mini-muffin pan, a regular muffin pan and a king-size muffin pan and you'll then be equipped to bake any of the muffin recipes in this book.

Convection oven temperature conversions

Regular oven	Convection oven
170°C/325°F	140°C
180°C/350°F	160°C
190°C/375°F	170°C
200°C/400°F	180°C
220°C/425°F	200°C
230°C/450°F	210°C

Cooking in a convection oven is generally 25% faster than in a regular oven.

Troubleshooting

Although I've tested and re-tested all the recipes in this book to make sure they work, there's always a chance that the end result might not meet your expectations. If you think something has gone wrong, check out the possible causes and solutions below.

Underbaked and slightly sunken?
It is likely that the oven had not reached the correct temperature before the muffins or scones were put in the oven. Always preheat the oven at the beginning of a recipe and put the goodies in to bake only when the light goes out, indicating the correct temperature has been reached.

How to fix it: If you realize that the muffins are under-cooked and sinking within 30 minutes of taking them out of the oven, you could return them to the hot oven and cook for a few more minutes. If you don't realize for an hour or so, try microwaving a few at a time. Cook on high (850w) for 1 minute. Let stand for a couple of minutes, then test with a toothpick—it should come out clean.

Overbaked?
Was the oven temperature set correctly? Did you use the right size muffin pans and not smaller cupcake pans? If you have a convection oven, you need to adjust the temperature accordingly, baking 20°C lower than a regular oven (see oven temperatures chart opposite). Or perhaps your oven is 10 or 20 degrees hotter than the dial indicates. If you find things regularly burn, call out a service engineer from the manufacturer—they can test your oven to check that it is correctly calibrated.

How to fix it: How overbaked are they? Burned tops need to be cut off. Disguise with icing, melted chocolate, or cream cheese frosting. If they're not burned, but just a little dry, pierce a few times with a toothpick and drizzle some fruit juice or alcohol over sweet muffins. Drizzle savory muffins with olive oil.

Crusty top?
This is usually caused if you've used too much sugar. Did you measure it carefully? Did you measure the corn syrup accurately? Digital scales that you can set to zero with each ingredient make adding ingredients directly to the mixing bowl easier. Also, use a measuring spoon dipped in hot water to make sure the syrup doesn't cling to the spoon.

How to fix it: Dust the tops with confectioners' sugar to taste like an intentional sugary crust.

Fruit sank?
Did you gently toss the fruit in the flour before adding the wet ingredients? This is a critical stage. Also, was the oven preheated to the correct temperature? If it is too low, the mixture does not set quickly enough to support the fruit while the mixture bakes.

How to fix it: Nothing you can do, but remember these hints for next time.

Muffin tops cracked and not baked through?
This is caused when the oven is too hot, so the top bakes quickly and sets before the lower part of the muffin has cooked, then during baking the mixture underneath forces its way up as it bakes and rises, splitting the already set surface.

How to fix it: Dust with confectioners' sugar.

Flat tops that didn't rise properly?

Did you remember to put in the correct amount of raising agent ? Measure baking powder and baking soda carefully with a measuring spoon—exact quantities are critical for the muffins to rise successfully. Also check the packets to ensure that the raising agents haven't passed their use-by date.

How to fix it: Cover with icing and call them cupcakes!

Muffins too crumbly?

If the mixture is quite stiff when it goes in to bake, the end result will probably be dry and crumbly. Measure liquids and fats carefully. If the texture is too crumbly, not enough liquid was added.

How to fix it: Drizzle with a lemon sugar syrup, alcohol, or fruit juice.

Oily texture?

Did you use butter or the oil suggested in the recipe? It sounds like you tried to use a lowfat spread or margarine. These contain water, and have the weird effect of separating out during cooking and making the muffin texture oily.

How to fix it: Serve with tangy fruit for sweet muffins or a crisp vinegar-dressed salad for savory ones.

Dense texture?

Sounds like you may have overmixed. Stir the wet and dry ingredients together for about ten strokes until everything is just combined. Don't overmix.

How to fix it: Microwave individual muffins and serve warm, like a pudding. Serve with ice cream or custard to disguise.

Seriously sunken? (pictured)

You've added too much raising agent. Use measuring spoons for accuracy.

How to fix it: Put some raspberries on top!

Mixture overflows?

Did you use large eggs instead of medium? (All recipes use medium eggs unless large are specified.) Have you used the correct size of muffin pan?

How to fix it: Make sure next time you only spoon enough muffin mixture into the liners or pan cups so that they are two-thirds full.

Cooked unevenly?

Are some of the muffins browned, while others are not? Sounds like your oven is cooking unevenly.

How to fix it: Next time, turn muffins round after 10–15 minutes cooking time, but don't open the oven door too soon, or they'll sink.

Muffins sticking to pans?

Did you grease them thoroughly? Use butter or corn oil and make sure you smear it right into the corners. Were you too impatient getting them out of the pans? Leave in the pans for 10 minutes to cool and firm up—if you try to remove them too soon, they'll be too fragile and break up. However, if you leave them too long they may well set in the pans.

How to fix it: Ideally use a nonstick pan, or a flexible plastic one. Use a palette knife to ease around the sides of each muffin and gently slip underneath to release. Or use paper muffin liners every time—they make life a lot easier.

Brilliant for Breakfast

Baking something for breakfast may sound like I'm living in fantasy-land. I know people lead busy lives and there's barely enough time to grab a slice of toast most days. What about weekends or birthdays or when you have friends to stay? If you're more energetic in the evenings than mornings, weigh out the ingredients before you go to bed and then, on the following day, turn on the oven, mix together the ingredients, and in no time you can tuck into warm, homebaked delights. And once you've made a batch, extras can be frozen and microwaved individually as and when you fancy a treat.

Whole-grain honey muffins

Just because these look like cakes doesn't mean they're going to taste like cakes! They're nothing like any store-bought, super-sweet specimen—in fact, they're almost as savory as a good old-fashioned slice of toast.

1 Heat the oven to 400°F/200°C. Line a muffin pan with 9 muffin liners.
2 Tip the flour into a large bowl. Add the baking powder and sugar.
3 Mix together the honey, oil, egg, lemon zest, and milk and pour into the dry ingredients in the bowl. Use a large spoon to fold everything together.
4 Spoon equally into the paper muffin liners and bake for 15 minutes, or until the muffins are well risen, firm, and springy to the touch. Serve warm.

MAKES 9 / READY IN 30 MINUTES

1⅓ cups malt or multi-grain flour
1 tbsp baking powder
⅛ cup dark brown sugar
3 tbsp honey
scant ½ cup sunflower oil
1 egg
finely grated zest of 1 small lemon
⅔ cup skim milk

Four-seed muffins

Bursting with goodness—what better way to start your day?

1 Heat the oven to 400°F/200°C. Line a 12-cup muffin pan with paper muffin liners.
2 Sift the self-rising flour into a large bowl. Add the whole-wheat flour, baking powder, all the seeds, raisins, and sugar.
3 Mix together the oil, egg, and milk and pour into the dry ingredients in the bowl. Stir together with a large spoon until just combined.
4 Spoon equally into the paper muffin liners and sprinkle with a fine dusting of your chosen seeds.
5 Bake for 15 minutes, or until the muffins are well risen, firm, and springy to the touch. Serve warm.

MAKES 12 / READY IN 30 MINUTES

generous ¾ cup self-rising white flour
⅔ cup stone-ground whole-wheat flour
1 tbsp baking powder
2oz | 50g mixture of poppy, sesame, sunflower, and pumpkin seeds
⅔ cup raisins
generous ⅓ cup dark brown sugar
scant ½ cup sunflower oil
1 egg
⅔ cup skim milk
extra seeds, for dusting

Apricot and oat muffins

These are great for freezing (see Cook's tip below), so make a batch of 12, then eat a few and freeze the remainder.

MAKES 12 / READY IN 30 MINUTES

generous ¾ cup self-rising white flour

scant ⅔ cup whole-wheat flour

1 tbsp baking powder

1 cup rolled oats

1 cup dried apricots, chopped

⅔ cup golden raisins

generous ⅓ cup dark brown sugar

scant ½ cup sunflower oil

1 egg

finely grated zest and juice of 1 orange

⅔ cup skim milk

extra rolled oats, for sprinkling

1 Heat the oven to 400°F/200°C. Line a 12-cup muffin pan with paper muffin liners.

2 Sift the self-rising flour into a large bowl. Add the whole-wheat flour, baking powder, rolled oats, apricots, golden raisins, and sugar.

3 Mix together the oil, egg, orange zest, juice, and milk and pour into the dry ingredients in the bowl. Use a large spoon to fold everything together.

4 Spoon equally into the paper muffin liners and sprinkle with oats.

5 Bake for 15 minutes, or until the muffins are well risen, firm, and springy to the touch. Serve warm.

Cook's tip: To freeze the muffins, cool completely and pack in small plastic bags. To serve, microwave on high (850w) for 40 seconds to warm through one muffin.

Whole-wheat apple

Try these for a tasty yet healthy high-fiber start to the day.

MAKES 12 / READY IN 30 MINUTES

½ cup self-rising white flour

scant 1 cup whole-wheat flour

1 tbsp baking powder

½ tsp ground cinnamon

½ cup chopped dried apples

generous ½ cup golden raisins

scant ½ cup dark brown sugar

scant ½ cup sunflower oil

1 egg

⅔ cup skim milk

2 tbsp rolled oats, for sprinkling

1 Heat the oven to 400°F/200°C. Line a 12-cup muffin pan with paper muffin liners.

2 Sift the self-rising flour into a large bowl. Add the whole-wheat flour, baking powder, cinnamon, apples, golden raisins, and sugar.

3 Mix together the oil, egg, and milk and pour into the dry ingredients in the bowl.

Use a large spoon to mix everything together until just combined.

4 Spoon equally into the paper muffin liners and sprinkle with oats.

5 Bake for 15 minutes, or until the muffins are well risen, firm, and springy to the touch. Serve warm.

English muffins

These traditional muffins are entirely different to American-style muffins baked in paper liners. The recipe uses a yeast dough, so they take longer to make. I've used active dry yeast to save a little time, or see the Cook's tips for using a bread machine. These are traditionally served at teatime, but I think they make a really special treat for breakfast.

MAKES 8–10 / READY IN 1 HOUR 15 MINUTES

3 cups white bread flour
1 tsp salt
¼ cup butter, plus extra for greasing
¼ oz envelope active dry yeast
1 tsp superfine sugar
1 cup warm milk

1 Sift the flour and salt into a bowl. Microwave on medium (500W) for 1 minute, to warm slightly (there's no need to warm the flour if you don't have a microwave—it simply helps the yeast to work faster).

2 Melt the butter in a bowl in the microwave for 50 seconds on high (850w), or in a pan.

3 Add the active dry yeast and sugar to the warm flour. Pour in the warm milk and butter.

4 Beat well until smooth and elastic. Cover and let rise in a warm place for 30 minutes or until doubled in size.

5 Turn onto a well-floured board and knead, working in a little more flour if necessary to make the dough easier to shape. Round up the dough, then roll into a thick sausage shape and (using the sharpest knife you have) slice into 8–10 portions, each about 1½in | 3cm thick.

6 Use a plain cutter to help shape each one into a round with straight sides. Place on a greased baking sheet, well spaced out. Cover with greased plastic wrap and put in a warm place to prove for 30–40 minutes, or until springy to the touch.

7 Heat a grill pan until really hot, then grease lightly with butter. Lift the muffins carefully onto the hot grill. Cook a few at a time over very low heat for 8–10 minutes, or until pale golden underneath. Turn and cook the other side.

8 Wrap in a cloth and keep warm if cooking in batches. To serve, insert a knife in the side and pull the top and bottom slightly apart, then insert slivers of butter.

Cook's tips

• Mix the dough with a heavy-duty electric mixer or, if you have a bread machine, you can just use it to knead and prove dough, then you can shape and bake it conventionally.

• Let the dough rise in a warm place, such as on the stove while the oven's on.

• Speed up the proving by microwaving the dough on defrost for 2 minutes.

• Freeze half the shaped dough before baking. Bake from frozen (just add a few more minutes to the cooking time).

How to adapt recipes for a bread machine:

Check your manufacturer's directions, as there is usually a very specific order in which you must add the ingredients to the bread bucket. Adding the ingredients in the wrong order could cause the recipe to fail. Most machines need liquid added first, followed by dry ingredients, then yeast. Confusingly, a few models use the reverse order. This is important for machines that have a rest time before the cycle starts, as the yeast must be kept separate from the liquid, sugar, and salt.

Bacon, cheese, and maple syrup

I love the traditional American breakfast—wonderfully indulgent, and combining both savory and sweet flavors on one plate. Try these muffins, and I bet you'll become hooked.

MAKES 8 / READY IN 30 MINUTES

4 slices smoked Canadian bacon, chopped
scant 1¼ cups self-rising flour
1 tsp baking powder
¼ tsp salt
½ cup grated sharp cheddar cheese
5 tbsp sunflower oil
1 egg
4 tbsp maple syrup
⅔ cup skim milk

1 Heat the oven to 400°F/200°C. Line a muffin pan with 8 paper liners.
2 Microwave the bacon uncovered on an ovenproof plate on high (850w) for 3 minutes until cooked and becoming crispy. (Or dry-roast in a nonstick frying pan.)
3 Sift the flour, baking powder, and salt into a bowl. Stir in the bacon and cheese. Make a well in the center.
4 Pour the oil, egg, half the maple syrup, and the milk into a pitcher and mix together, then pour into the well, in the center. Mix together briefly until just combined.
5 Spoon the mixture into the prepared muffin liners and bake for 15 minutes, or until risen, firm, and a toothpick inserted into the center comes out clean.
6 Serve warm, drizzled with the remaining maple syrup.

Cook's tip: Cool and freeze for up to 1 month. Defrost one muffin at a time in the microwave on high (850W) for 40 seconds.

Muesli muffins

Wholesome and satisfying served just as they are.

MAKES 9 / READY IN 30 MINUTES

⅓ cup self-rising white flour
scant ½ cup whole-wheat flour
2 tsp baking powder
⅔ cup fruit-and-nut muesli
scant ⅓ cup raisins
scant ½ cup dark brown sugar
scant ½ cup sunflower oil
1 egg
⅔ cup skim milk
extra muesli, for dusting

1 Heat the oven to 400°F/200°C. Line a muffin pan with 9 paper muffin liners.
2 Sift the self-rising flour into a large bowl. Add the whole-wheat flour, baking powder, muesli, raisins, and sugar.
3 Mix together the oil, egg, and milk in a pitcher, then pour into the dry ingredients in the bowl. Use a large metal spoon to fold everything together.
4 Spoon evenly into the paper muffin liners, then sprinkle with the extra muesli and bake for 15 minutes, or until the muffins are well risen, firm, and springy to the touch. Serve warm.

Smoked salmon and chive

For a very refined yet substantial breakfast, try these muffins served with scrambled eggs. Alternatively, bake them as mini-muffins and serve them with pre-dinner drinks or as part of a buffet.

1 Heat the oven to 400°F/200°C. Line a muffin pan with 9 paper muffin liners (or line mini-muffin pans with 24 mini-muffin paper liners).
2 Sift the flour, baking powder, and salt into a bowl. Stir in the smoked salmon, chives, and cheese. Make a well in the center.

3 Pour the oil, egg, mustard, and milk into the well. Mix together briefly until just combined.
4 Spoon the mixture into the prepared muffin liners and bake for 12 minutes, or until risen, firm, and a toothpick inserted into the center comes out clean. (Mini-muffins should be baked for 7 minutes.)

MAKES 9, OR 24 MINI-MUFFINS / READY IN 30 MINUTES

1½ cups self-rising flour

1 tsp baking powder

¼ tsp salt

3oz | 75g smoked salmon trimmings, chopped

1 tbsp freshly chopped chives, optional

¼ cup grated Parmesan cheese

5 tbsp sunflower oil

1 egg, lightly beaten

1 tbsp whole-grain mustard

⅔ cup skim milk

Marmalade orange muffins

Split and fill these with a dollop of marmalade, if you crave that extra degree of sweetness, to start your day.

1 Heat the oven to 400°F/200°C. Line a 12-cup muffin pan with paper muffin liners.
2 Sift the self-rising flour into a large bowl. Add the malted brown flour, baking powder, and sugar.
3 Mix together the marmalade, oil, egg, orange zest, juice, and milk and pour into the dry ingredients in the bowl. Use a large metal spoon to fold everything together.

4 Spoon equally into the paper muffin liners.
5 Bake for 15 minutes, or until the muffins are well risen, firm, and springy to the touch. Serve warm.

Cook's tip: To freeze the muffins, cool completely and pack in small plastic bags. To defrost, microwave one muffin at a time on high (850w) for 30 seconds.

MAKES 12 / READY IN 30 MINUTES

1 cup self-rising white flour

scant 1 cup malt or multi-grain flour

1 tbsp baking powder

scant ½ cup dark brown sugar

⅓ cup marmalade

scant ½ cup sunflower oil

1 egg

finely grated zest and juice of 1 orange

5 tbsp skim milk

Bran and banana muffins

These muffins are high in fiber and satisfyingly filling, with a gorgeous caramelly flavor. If you can get hold of muscovado sugar, an unrefined brown sugar that comes directly from sugar cane, you'll really taste the difference.

1 Preheat the oven to 400°F/200°C. Line a 12-cup muffin pan with paper muffin liners.
2 Mix the flour, bran, sugar, baking powder, salt, and raisins together in a bowl.
3 In a pitcher lightly whisk together the milk, egg, and oil with a fork. Pour the wet ingredients onto the dry ingredients and gently stir together until just blended.
4 Mash up the bananas with a fork and add to the muffin mixture. Don't overmix.
5 Spoon the mixture evenly into the muffin liners and bake for 20–25 minutes, or until a toothpick inserted into the center of one comes out clean.

MAKES 12 / READY IN 35 MINUTES

scant 1¼ cups whole-wheat flour
1 cup bran
3 tbsp soft dark brown sugar
2 tsp baking powder
pinch of salt
scant ⅔ cup raisins
⅔ cup milk
1 large egg
5 tbsp sunflower oil
2 ripe bananas, peeled (225g | 8oz peeled weight)

Children's Choice

Yes, we all know children love sweet things, but that doesn't mean we need to pump them full of artificial sweeteners, colorings, and additives to present them with fun food. These muffins will help satisfy their cravings for something special without compromising your food standards. Because many of these may well be made for birthday parties, or for when friends come round, I've kept the muffin size small. Why waste big muffins on little appetites when you can make them mini? If they're a hit, the children can come back for more.

Chocolate chip muffins

Let your imagination go to give you endless variations on this recipe. Although I suggest chocolate chips, why not substitute your favorite chocolate of the moment. If you like chocolates with a honeycomb center or gooey toffee, they're worth a try. Cut them into tiny chunks, the size of your little fingernail (you may find it less messy doing this if they've been chilled a little first), then you can be the judge of how successful your choice is.

MAKES 12 SMALL CUPCAKE- SIZED MUFFINS / READY IN 30 MINUTES

1 cup all-purpose flour
1 tsp baking powder
scant ½ cup sugar
⅓ cup milk chocolate chips
⅔ cup sour cream
1 egg
4 tbsp sunflower oil

1 Preheat the oven to 375°F/190°C. Line a 12-cup regular muffin pan with paper liners.
2 Sift the flour and baking powder into a bowl and add the sugar and chocolate chips and stir to combine.
3 Put the sour cream, egg, and sunflower oil into a pitcher and mix together with a fork until smooth.

4 Stir the wet ingredients into the dry until just combined.
5 Spoon the mixture into the paper liners, so that each liner is only half full, and bake for 6-8 minutes, or until the muffins are well risen, pale golden, and a toothpick inserted into the center comes out clean.

Crunchy peanut butter muffins

Before you offer these to any children, do check that they're not allergic to nuts.

MAKES 24 MINI-MUFFINS / READY IN 25 MINUTES

1 cup all-purpose flour
1 tsp baking powder
½ cup superfine sugar
pinch of salt
6 tbsp crunchy peanut butter
scant ½ cup sunflower oil
1 large egg
¾ cup skim milk

1 Preheat the oven to 400°F/200°C. Line mini-muffin pans with 24 paper mini-muffin liners.
2 Sift the flour, baking powder, sugar, and salt together into a bowl.
3 In a large pitcher mix the peanut butter, oil, egg, and milk together with a fork.

4 Pour the wet ingredients into the dry, then stir gently together to combine.
5 Spoon into the paper muffin liners. Bake for 7 minutes, or until the muffins are firm, risen, and golden, and a toothpick inserted into the center comes out clean.

Banana and honey muffins

This is a great way to use up overripe bananas. Because the bananas are squishy, you can get away with not using any eggs.

1 Heat the oven to 375°F/190°C. Line 24 mini-muffin pans with paper mini-muffin liners.
2 Sift the flour, baking powder, baking soda, and cinnamon into a bowl.
3 In a large pitcher, mix together the oil, honey, and milk with a fork.
4 Pour the wet ingredients onto the dry and gently stir together with the mashed bananas.

5 Spoon into the mini-muffin liners and bake for 8–10 minutes, or until risen and firm.
6 Eat whilst warm or cool on a wire rack.

Cook's tip: Whiz up the bananas with a hand blender for a speedy way to make them really smooth.

MAKES 24 MINI-MUFFINS / READY IN 30 MINUTES

1 cup all-purpose flour
1½ tsp baking powder
½ tsp baking soda
¼ tsp ground cinnamon
⅓ cup sunflower oil
4 tbsp honey
¼ cup lowfat milk
2 small ripe bananas, peeled and mashed (5½oz | 150g peeled weight)

Chocolate muffins

These have a sweeter taste rather than being really chocolatey, and are so easy that children can make them too.

1 Preheat the oven to 400°F/200°C. Line regular muffin pans with 17 paper liners.
2 Melt the butter in a pitcher in the microwave for 50 seconds on high (850w), or in a pan over low heat.
3 Sift together the flour, cocoa, and baking powder into a bowl. Add the sugar and salt.
4 Add the egg and yogurt to the melted butter and mix with a fork. Mix the wet ingredients with the dry.

5 Spoon into the paper liners. Each should be about half full. Bake for 10–15 minutes, or until the muffins are risen and firm.
6 Cool the muffins on a wire rack. When cool, top with chocolate spread and smooth over to cover. Sprinkle with colored sprinkles to finish.

MAKES 17 SMALL CUPCAKE-SIZED MUFFINS / READY IN 25 MINUTES

scant ½ cup butter
1½ cups all-purpose flour
2 tbsp unsweetened cocoa
1 tbsp baking powder
generous ½ cup dark brown sugar
pinch of salt
1 large egg
1¼ cups plain yogurt
6 tbsp chocolate spread
3 tbsp chocolate-flavored colored sprinkles

Coconut muffins

These coconut muffins are topped with a smothering of jelly and a scattering of shredded sweetened coconut. The ordinary dry unsweetened variety would do, but it doesn't have quite the same "yum" factor. As an alternative, top the finished muffins with chocolate spread instead of jelly before crowning them with a sprinkling from tropical heaven.

MAKES 24 MINI-MUFFINS / READY IN 30 MINUTES

1 cup all-purpose flour

1 tsp baking powder

scant ½ cup superfine sugar

generous ½ cup shredded sweetened coconut

⅔ cup tropical-flavored yogurt

1 egg

4 tbsp sunflower oil

To decorate:

3 tbsp strawberry jelly

3 tbsp sweetened shredded coconut

1 Heat the oven to 375°F/190°C. Line mini-muffin pans with 24 paper mini-muffin liners.

2 Sift the flour and baking powder into a bowl, then add the sugar and sweetened tenderized coconut and stir to combine.

3 Put the tropical yogurt, egg, and sunflower oil into a pitcher and mix together with a fork until smooth.

4 Stir the wet ingredients into the dry until just combined.

5 Spoon the mixture into the paper muffin liners and bake for 6–8 minutes, or until the muffins are well risen, pale golden, and firm.

6 Brush over the strawberry jelly while warm and sprinkle over the remaining sweetened tenderized coconut, to decorate.

Lemon curd muffins

If you splurge on a slightly more expensive, better quality brand of lemon curd, it'll be worth it, as the muffins will have a more defined lemony flavor that even children will detect. These are fabulous eaten warm.

MAKES 12 SMALL CUPCAKE-SIZED MUFFINS / READY IN 30 MINUTES

1⅓ cups self-rising flour

½ cup superfine sugar

1 large egg

5 tbsp sunflower oil

⅔ cup milk

½ tsp vanilla extract

4 tbsp lemon curd

For the sugar coating:

4 tbsp lemon curd

¼ cup superfine sugar

1 Heat the oven to 375°F/190°C. Line a 12-cup regular muffin pan with paper liners.

2 Sift the flour into a bowl and stir in the sugar.

3 In a large pitcher mix together the egg, sunflower oil, milk, and vanilla extract, using a fork.

4 Pour the wet ingredients into the dry and stir gently together until just combined.

5 Put a teaspoonful of the mixture in the base of each paper liner. Top with 1 tsp lemon curd. Top with the rest of the muffin mixture. Each liner should only be half full.

6 Bake for 10–15 minutes, or until risen and firm.

7 For the sugar coating, microwave the lemon curd on high (850w) for 1 minute until melted. Put the sugar into a shallow bowl. Brush on top of each muffin and dip the top of each one in the sugar to coat the tops.

Pink fairy muffins

These fairy dust-topped buns are such a pretty shade of pink, yet there's not a smidgen of food coloring in sight.

1 Heat the oven to 375°F/190°C. Line a 12-cup mini-muffin pan with paper mini-muffin liners.
2 Sift the flour and baking powder into a bowl, then add the sugar and dried cherries and stir to combine.
3 Put the strawberry yogurt, jelly, egg, and sunflower oil into a pitcher and mix together with a fork until smooth.

4 Stir the wet ingredients into the dry until just combined.
5 Spoon the mixture into the paper liners and bake for 6–8 minutes, or until the muffins are firm and well risen.
6 Mix together the jelly and granulated sugar and sprinkle on top of each muffin to look like fairy dust.
7 Decorate with a mini paper fairy secured onto a toothpick.

MAKES 12 MINI-MUFFINS / READY IN 30 MINUTES

1 cup all-purpose flour
1 tsp baking powder
scant ½ cup superfine sugar
⅓ cup dried sour cherries
⅔ cup strawberry yogurt
1 tbsp strawberry jelly
1 egg
4 tbsp sunflower oil

To decorate:
4 tsp strawberry jelly
3 tbsp granulated sugar

Marbled soccer muffins

Fantasy food for little boys. There's no food coloring in these, either, to make those boisterous chaps uncontrollable.

1 Heat the oven to 375°F/190°C. Line a 12-cup mini-muffin pan with paper liners.
2 Sift the flour and baking powder into a bowl. Add the sugar and stir to combine.
3 Put the egg and sunflower oil into a pitcher and mix with a fork until smooth.
4 Pour the contents of the pitcher into the dry ingredients and stir until just combined.
5 Divide the mixture between two bowls. Stir half the ricotta, the melted dark chocolate and the cocoa into one bowl and the remaining ricotta into the other bowl.

6 Spoon a dollop of each mixture alternately into the muffin liners and bake for 6–8 minutes, or until the muffins are firm and well risen.
7 Melt the white chocolate in a bowl over simmering water or microwave on medium (500w) for 2 minutes. Pour the melted chocolate over the cooled muffins.
8 Arrange the chocolate chips or buttons on top of each muffin.

MAKES 12 MINI-MUFFINS / READY IN 30 MINUTES

1 cup all-purpose flour
1 tsp baking powder
scant ½ cup superfine sugar
1 egg, lightly beaten
4 tbsp sunflower oil
⅔ cup ricotta cheese
2 tbsp melted dark chocolate
2 tsp cocoa

To decorate:
3½ squares white chocolate
milk chocolate chips or chocolate buttons

Jelly surprise muffins

There's something almost donutty about these muffins with their jelly centers. For the best results, eat them warm.

MAKES 12 SMALL CUPCAKE- SIZED MUFFINS / READY IN 30 MINUTES

1⅓ cups self-rising flour
½ cup superfine sugar
1 large egg
5 tbsp sunflower oil
⅔ cup milk
½ tsp vanilla extract
8 tsp strawberry jelly

For the sugar coating:
2 tbsp unsalted butter, melted
2 tbsp superfine sugar

1 Heat the oven to 375°F/190°C. Line a 12-cup regular muffin pan with paper liners. Next sift the flour into a bowl and stir in the sugar.

2 In a large pitcher mix together the egg, sunflower oil, milk and vanilla extract, using a fork.

3 Pour the wet ingredients into the dry and stir gently together until just combined.

4 Put a teaspoonful of the mixture in the base of each paper liner. Top each one with a dollop of strawberry jelly and then the rest of the muffin mixture. The liners should only be half full.

5 Bake for 10 minutes, or until well risen and firm.

6 Put the sugar in a shallow bowl. Brush the tops with melted butter and dip in the sugar to coat the tops.

Squashed fly muffins

I fall into the group who think of dried fruit as the cherry on top of the cake; something of a treat to savor. My children don't feel the same way as I do and tend to think of anything containing raisins as a penalty you have to pick through to get to the bit you really want to eat. So that's why I've called them "squashed fly" muffins, to make them more fun!

MAKES 12 SMALL CUPCAKE- SIZED MUFFINS / READY IN 30 MINUTES

1 cup all-purpose flour
1 tsp baking powder
scant ½ cup superfine sugar
scant ⅓ cup raisins
⅔ cup your favorite flavored yogurt
1 egg
4 tbsp sunflower oil

1 Heat the oven to 375°F/190°C. Line a 12-cup regular muffin pan with paper liners.

2 Sift the flour and baking powder into a bowl and add the sugar and raisins and stir to combine.

3 Put the yogurt, egg, and sunflower oil into a pitcher and mix together with a fork until smooth.

4 Stir the wet ingredients into the dry until just combined.

5 Spoon the mixture into the paper muffin liners, filling each one only about half way, and bake for 6–8 minutes, or until the muffins are well risen and firm.

Classic Combinations

Some of my favorite recipes are traditional ones. Although I enjoy experimenting with new ingredients and flavor combinations, I don't like adding new or unnecessary ingredients just for the sake of it. If you can make a perfectly good muffin with ten ingredients, why use 14? That's the approach I've taken with the recipes in this chapter—they're tried, tested, and trusted family favorites. They're the sort of muffins that don't cost a fortune to make and would go down really well at a school bake sale.

Lemon and poppy seed muffins

Poppy seeds not only add an interesting texture to these muffins but also have added health benefits. Just 1 tbsp of poppy seeds a day gives you more than 10 percent of your daily calcium requirement.

1 Preheat the oven to 400°F/200°C. Line a 12-cup muffin pan with paper muffin liners.

2 In a large pitcher mix together the sunflower oil, sugar, eggs, yogurt, lemon zest and juice, and poppy seeds.

3 Put the flour and baking soda into a bowl, then pour on the wet ingredients but do not overmix.

4 Spoon the mixture into the paper muffin liners and bake for 15 minutes, or until well risen and firm.

MAKES 12 / READY IN 30 MINUTES

scant ½ cup sunflower oil

½ cup superfine sugar

2 eggs

1 cup plain yogurt

finely grated zest and juice of 2 lemons

3oz | 75g poppy seeds

2 cups self-rising flour

½ tsp baking soda

Sticky ginger and corn syrup muffins

These moist muffins will keep for up to five days if stored in a cool place in a sealed container.

1 Preheat the oven to 400°F/200°C. Line a 12-cup muffin pan with paper muffin liners.

2 Sift the flour, baking soda, allspice, and ginger into a bowl.

3 In a pitcher mix together the oil, corn syrup, brown sugar, eggs, and milk.

4 Pour the wet ingredients into the dry, then gently mix them together. Spoon the mixture into the muffin liners and bake for 10–15 minutes, or until well risen and firm.

MAKES 12 / READY IN 25 MINUTES

1⅓ cups self-rising flour

½ tsp baking soda

1 tsp allspice

1 tbsp ground ginger

scant ½ cup sunflower oil

scant ⅓ cup dark corn syrup

½ cup dark brown sugar

2 eggs

generous ¾ cup milk

Buttery vanilla muffins

With just a handful of ingredients in these muffins, you can really appreciate how good plain muffins are. These are best enjoyed on the day they are made, so why not bake half a dozen and freeze the remainder unbaked? They'll take 25 minutes to cook from frozen.

1 Preheat the oven to 400°F/200°C. Line a 12-cup muffin pan with paper muffin liners.
2 Melt the butter in a bowl in the microwave for 50 seconds on high (850w), or in a pan.
3 Mix the flour, baking soda, baking powder, and sugar together in a bowl.
4 Mix together the egg, sour cream, melted butter, and vanilla extract, then pour into the dry ingredients and stir.

5 Spoon the mixture into the muffin liners and bake for 15 minutes, or until pale golden, risen and firm.
Cook's tip: If you have about 3¹⁄₂oz | 100g of fruit you'd like to use up, try adding it, chopped, to the mixture with the flour. Well-drained canned fruit works just as well as fresh. Try apricots, peaches, pineapple, mandarins, strawberries, rhubarb, raspberries, blackcurrants, or cherries. Toss the fruit into the flour first to prevent it sinking during baking.

MAKES 12 / READY IN 30 MINUTES
6 tbsp butter
1¹⁄₃ cups all-purpose flour
¹⁄₂ tsp baking soda
2 tsp baking powder
generous ¹⁄₂ cup superfine sugar
1 large egg
scant 1¹⁄₄ cups sour cream
1 tbsp vanilla extract

Apple and cinnamon crumble muffins

The pecans, cinnamon, and sugar give these an interesting crunchy crust.

1 Preheat the oven to 375°F/190°C. Line a 12-cup muffin pan with paper muffin liners.
2 Put the flour, superfine sugar, baking powder, ¹⁄₂ tsp cinnamon, and salt into a bowl.
3 Add the egg, milk, apple, and oil and stir for a few seconds until just combined.

4 Spoon the mixture into the paper muffin liners.
5 Put the pecans into a processor and whiz to chop finely, then add the dark brown sugar and the remaining cinnamon. Sprinkle over each muffin.
6 Bake for 15–20 minutes, or until well risen and firm. Serve warm.

MAKES 12 / READY IN 35 MINUTES
1¹⁄₂ cups all-purpose flour
scant ¹⁄₂ cup superfine sugar
2 tsp baking powder
1 tsp cinnamon
pinch of salt
1 egg
²⁄₃ cup lowfat milk
2 apples, peeled, cored, and finely chopped
¹⁄₄ cup sunflower oil
scant ¹⁄₄ cup pecans
¹⁄₄ cup dark brown sugar

Mincemeat and rum muffins

Try these as an easy alternative to mince pies. There's no need to limit them to Christmas-time only, as the mincemeat adds a lovely moistness to the muffins, which also helps them keep fresh for several days in an airtight container.

MAKES 12 / READY IN 35 MINUTES

¼ cup butter

2⅓ cups all-purpose flour

¼ cup superfine sugar

2 tsp baking powder

⅔ cup apple juice

2 eggs

9oz | 250g fruit mincemeat

12 sugar cubes

3 tbsp rum

1 Preheat the oven to 375°F/190°C. Line a 12-cup muffin pan with paper muffin liners.
2 Melt the butter in a bowl in the microwave for 50 seconds on high (850w), or in a pan.
3 Combine the flour, superfine sugar, and baking powder in a bowl and mix well.
4 Pour the melted butter into a pitcher with the apple juice and eggs. Beat together well with a fork.

5 Stir the liquid ingredients into the dry mixture, then add the mincemeat and stir until just moistened. Spoon the mixture into muffin liners.
6 Put the sugar cubes into a shallow bowl. Pour over the rum to soak, then put one on top of each muffin.
7 Bake for 15–20 minutes, or until well risen and firm.

Cheese and chutney muffins

Who doesn't enjoy a large chunk of cheese served with pickle or chutney? Why not combine the two in these scrumptious savory muffins and serve them with some crunchy carrot and celery stalks—they're perfect for a packed lunch.

MAKES 12 / READY IN 40 MINUTES

¼ cup butter, plus extra for greasing

1 egg

1 cup milk

1 tsp English or French mustard

3 tbsp chutney or pickle

1⅛ cups grated sharp cheddar cheese

1 tbsp baking powder

2 cups all-purpose flour

¼ tsp salt

1 Preheat the oven to 375°F/190°C. Grease a 12-cup muffin pan with butter.
2 Melt the butter in a bowl in the microwave for 50 seconds on high (850w), or in a pan.
3 Put the butter, egg, milk, mustard, and chutney into a large bowl and mix well.

4 Add the cheese, baking powder, flour, and salt. Stir together until just mixed.
5 Spoon into muffin pan and bake for 15–20 minutes, or until well risen and firm.

Cappuccino and chocolate chip

The perfect treat to go with your morning cup of espresso, latte, or cappuccino. If you like a stronger flavor, add an extra teaspoon of instant coffee to the muffin mixture. Use a decaffeinated variety if that's what you prefer.

MAKES 12 / READY IN 35 MINUTES

½ cup butter

2 cups all-purpose flour

¾ cup superfine sugar

2½ tsp baking powder

½ tsp salt

1 tbsp instant espresso coffee powder

½ tsp ground cinnamon

1 cup lowfat milk, heated and cooled

1 egg, lightly beaten

3½oz | 100g dark chocolate, cut into mini chunks (whiz in a blender for speed)

2 tbsp confectioners' sugar, sifted

1oz | 25g square dark chocolate, grated

1 Preheat the oven to 375°F/190°C. Line a 12-cup muffin pan with paper muffin liners.

2 Melt the butter in a bowl in the microwave for 50 seconds on high (850w), or in a pan.

3 In a large bowl, stir together the flour, sugar, baking powder, salt, instant coffee, and cinnamon.

4 In a pitcher stir together the milk, egg, and melted butter, until blended.

5 Pour the wet ingredients into the dry. Stir in the chocolate chunks.

6 Spoon the mixture into the paper muffin liners and bake for 15–20 minutes, or until well risen and firm.

7 Dust the muffins with confectioners' sugar and grated chocolate, if liked.

Banana and toffee muffins

These banana muffins are made extra special by the surprise toffee centers.

MAKES 12 / READY IN 30 MINUTES

6 tbsp butter

generous 1¾ cups self-rising flour

1 tsp baking soda

generous ½ cup dark brown sugar

3 large, ripe bananas (about 450g | 1lb)

1 large egg

¼ cup milk

12 fudge toffees

1 Heat the oven to 375°F/190°C. Line a 12-cup muffin pan with paper muffin liners.

2 Melt the butter in a bowl in the microwave for 50 seconds on high (850w), or in a pan.

3 Sift the flour and baking soda into a bowl. Add the sugar.

4 Mash the bananas with a fork and add to the bowl.

5 Crack the egg into a pitcher. Add the milk and melted butter and mix together with a fork.

6 Stir the wet ingredients into the dry and mix together until just combined.

7 Spoon half the mixture into the paper muffin liners. Top with a fudge toffee, then spoon over the remaining muffin mixture.

8 Bake for 15 minutes, or until they are well risen and firm.

Cook's tip: Toss the toffees in flour before adding them to stop them sinking during baking.

Carrot and cream cheese muffins

These muffins taste so good even without the cream cheese frosting, but it does provide a gorgeously gooey finishing touch.

1 Heat the oven to 400°F/200°C. Line a 12-cup muffin pan with 8 paper muffin liners.

2 Sift the flour, baking soda, cinnamon, and nutmeg into a bowl.

3 Pour the oil into a pitcher, then add the sour cream, sugar, and eggs and beat with a fork until well blended.

4 Pour the wet ingredients into the dry, then add the carrots and gently stir everything together to combine.

5 Spoon into the prepared muffin liners and bake for 15–20 minutes, or until well risen and firm. Let cool.

6 Mix together the butter and cream cheese until softened and combined. Stir in the confectioners' sugar and vanilla extract and mix together. Spread over the top of the cooled muffins.

MAKES 8 / READY IN 35 MINUTES

1½ cups self-rising flour

1 tsp baking soda

1 tsp ground cinnamon

½ tsp ground nutmeg

⅔ cup sunflower oil

⅔ cup sour cream

generous 1 cup superfine sugar

2 large eggs

4oz | 125g carrots, peeled and coarsely grated

For the frosting:

¼ cup butter

scant 1 cup cream cheese

½ cup unrefined confectioners' sugar

¼ tsp vanilla extract

Chocolate brownie muffins

There's a seriously large quantity of chocolate in these brownie muffins and that's what gives them their wicked fudgey centers. Many chefs suggest using dark chocolate that contains more than 70 percent cocoa solids, but although I love dark chocolate I think that would make these brownies too bitter. Use a bitter chocolate that has about 50 percent cocoa solids.

1 Preheat the oven to 375°F/190°C. Line a 12-cup muffin pan with paper muffin liners.

2 Put the chocolate and butter into a bowl and microwave on medium (500w) for 2 minutes. stir, then microwave on high (850w) for an additional 2 minutes, or until just melted. Alternatively, melt in a bowl over a pan of simmering water.

3 Sift the flour into a bowl and stir in the sugar.

4 Add the milk and eggs to the chocolate and mix together.

5 Pour the wet ingredients into the dry and stir together to combine.

6 Spoon into the paper muffin liners and bake for 20 minutes, or until risen and just firm.

MAKES 12 / READY IN 35 MINUTES

12oz | 350g dark chocolate (50% cocoa solids), broken into pieces

¾ cup butter

⅔ cup self-rising flour

generous 1 cup superfine sugar

3 tbsp milk

3 eggs

Something Savory

Think of these savory muffins as little flavored breads with a lovely texture. Fast and easy to make, they're so versatile that once you've mastered a few of these recipes (and been complimented for your innovative cooking), I'm sure you'll want to try more. They're great to serve as flavorsome nibbles to go with drinks—make them in mini-muffin pans instead of the regular size and you'll get 36 (just cook them for a slightly shorter time). Great for buffet parties too, or try them as an accompaniment for vegetable soups and salads.

Spicy tex-mex muffins

Cornmeal is made from milled corn or maize and adds an interesting texture to these muffins. Try serving these with guacamole, salsa, and salad with a sour cream dressing. They are best eaten within two days.

1 Preheat the oven to 375°F/190°C. Lightly grease a 12-cup muffin pan by brushing with oil or line the pan with paper muffin liners.
2 Tip the cornmeal, flour, salt, and baking powder into a large bowl.
3 In a pitcher, mix together the eggs, Tabasco, sunflower oil, and sour cream. Add this to the flour mixture and stir quickly to just combine.

4 Add the corn, goat cheese, chile, and cilantro and gently fold through.
5 Spoon into the muffin liners and bake for 15–20 minutes, or until well risen and firm.

Cook's tip: Wear rubber gloves when you seed and chop chiles to ensure you don't get spicy seeds stuck under your fingernails, as these could then irritate skin or eyes.

MAKES 12 / READY IN 35 MINUTES

oil to grease
⅔ cup cornmeal
½ cup all-purpose flour
pinch of salt
1 tbsp baking powder
2 large eggs
dash of Tabasco sauce
scant ½ cup sunflower oil
⅔ cup sour cream
1 cup corn
3½oz | 100g goat cheese, crumbled
1 red or green chile, seeded and chopped
2 tbsp freshly chopped cilantro leaves

Walnut, leek, and bacon muffins

Try these with a crunchy salad—watercress, romaine lettuce, celery, and apple with a mustard dressing would work well together.

1 Preheat the oven to 375°F/190°C. Grease a 12-cup muffin pan.
2 Microwave the bacon on high (850w) for 3 minutes until cooked or dry fry.
3 Put the leeks into a bowl with 1 tbsp of the butter and microwave on high (850w) for 3 minutes until softened, or cook in a pan over a gentle heat.
4 Melt the remaining butter in the microwave on high (850w) for 50 seconds, or melt in a pan. Put the eggs into a large pitcher with the butter and sour cream and mix together with a fork. Season with salt and freshly ground black pepper.

5 Put the walnuts in a processor and whiz to chop, then add the flour, paprika, baking powder, and half of the cheese. Blend together.
6 Pour in the wet ingredients, bacon, and leeks and blend for a few seconds, or until just combined.
7 Spoon the mixture into the prepared muffin pans and bake for 15 minutes. Sprinkle the rest of the cheese over the top of the muffins and bake for an additional 5–10 minutes, or until well risen and firm.

MAKES 12 / READY IN 40 MINUTES

4 strips smoked rindless bacon, chopped
1 small leek, finely chopped
6 tbsp butter
2 large eggs
⅔ cup sour cream
salt and freshly ground black pepper
1 cup walnuts
½ cup all-purpose flour
¼ tsp paprika
1 tsp baking powder
½ cup grated Emmental cheese

Mushroom and sunblush tomato muffins

Sunblush tomatoes are semi-dried tomatoes kept moist with olive oil. If you can't find them in the stores, try making your own by drizzling tomato halves with extra virgin olive oil and baking in a low oven until they begin to shrivel.

MAKES 12 / READY IN 30 MINUTES

1⅓ cups all-purpose flour

½ cup fine cornmeal

1 tsp salt

1 tbsp baking powder

4 sunblush or sun-dried tomatoes, drained from oil and chopped

1 cup sliced baby button mushrooms

½ cup grated pecorino cheese

3 eggs, lightly beaten

1¼ cups milk

4 tbsp light olive oil

1 Preheat the oven to 475°F/220°C. Line a 12-cup muffin pan with paper muffin liners.

2 Sift the flour into a large bowl and add the cornmeal, salt, and baking powder. Add the tomatoes, mushrooms, and cheese.

3 Mix together the eggs, milk, and oil with a fork. Pour the wet ingredients onto the dry and gently stir together to combine.

4 Spoon the mixture into the muffin liners, dividing equally.

5 Bake for 15 minutes, or until the muffins are well risen and firm.

Cook's tip: If these muffins are for a special occasion, try using soaked and chopped porcini mushrooms instead of the fresh mushrooms. They will give an intense flavor and will retain their firmness after cooking.

Sweet pepper and mozzarella cheese muffins

Roast your own bell pepper if you have time or look out for roasted marinated peppers sold in jars—they have a wonderful sweet flavor.

MAKES 9/ READY IN 1 HOUR

generous ¾ cup whole-wheat flour

generous ¾ cup all-purpose flour

⅓ cup cornmeal

1 tbsp superfine sugar

1 tbsp baking powder

pinch of salt

2 roasted sweet peppers, drained from oil and chopped

1 cup lowfat milk

2 large eggs

4 tbsp light olive oil

3oz | 75g mozzarella cheese, cubed

1 tbsp fresh basil leaves, torn

1 Preheat the oven to 375°F/190°C. Grease 9 cups of a muffin pan or line with paper muffin liners.

2 In a large bowl, combine the whole-wheat flour, all-purpose flour, polenta, sugar, baking powder, and salt. Add the pepper and stir to mix evenly.

3 Pour the milk, eggs, and the olive oil into a pitcher and whisk together with a fork. Pour into the flour mixture and stir with a large spatula just until moistened, using no more than 15–20 strokes. The batter will be lumpy.

4 Half-fill the muffin liners with the mixture and put a cube of mozzarella cheese and some basil in the center. Cover with the remaining mixture until mounded just level with the top of the pan.

5 Bake for 20–25 minutes, or until well risen and firm. Serve them warm.

Italian pizza muffins

This recipe was inspired by a classic salami, tomato, cheese, and garlic pizza.

MAKES 12 / READY IN 35 MINUTES

12 slices pepperoni

12 pitted olives

1⅔ cups all-purpose flour

1 tbsp baking powder

1 tsp freshly chopped oregano (dried will do)

¼ tsp paprika

6oz | 175g mozzarella cheese, grated

1 tomato, finely chopped

1 garlic clove, peeled and crushed

generous ¾ cup skim milk

2 eggs, beaten

4 tbsp olive oil

1 Preheat the oven to 375°F/190°C. Line a 12-cup muffin pan with paper muffin liners.

2 Cut the pepperoni slices in half. Set aside 12 halves and chop the remainder. Repeat for the olives.

3 Mix together the flour, baking powder, oregano, paprika, and most of the cheese in a large bowl. Add the diced pepperoni, olives, tomato, and garlic.

4 Pour the milk, eggs, and oil into a pitcher and mix together with a fork.

5 Add the wet ingredients to the dry ingredients, mixing until just combined.

6 Spoon the mixture into the muffin liners. Put a slice of pepperoni and an olive on top of each muffin and sprinkle with the remaining grated cheese. Bake for 15–20 minutes, or until well risen and firm.

Cornmeal and cheese muffins

Eat these on the day they're made or, better still, enjoy them warm. Perfect served with a steaming bowl of mushroom soup.

MAKES 9 / READY IN 30 MINUTES

1 cup all-purpose flour

1 cup polenta

2 tsp superfine sugar

1 tsp salt

1 tbsp baking powder

2 tsp coarsely ground black peppercorns

½ cup grated Parmesan cheese

2 eggs, lightly beaten

scant 1 cup skim milk

4 tbsp light olive oil

1 Preheat the oven to 475°F/220°C. Line 9 cups of a muffin pan with paper muffin liners.

2 Sift the flour into a large bowl and add the cornmeal, sugar, salt, baking powder, and ground peppercorns. Add ¼ cup of the cheese.

3 Mix together the eggs, milk, and olive oil with a fork. Pour the wet ingredients onto the dry and gently stir together to combine.

4 Spoon the mixture into the muffin liners, dividing equally. Sprinkle over the rest of the cheese.

5 Bake for 15 minutes, or until the muffins are well risen and firm.

Feta and olive muffins

These are perfect served alongside a big crunchy bowl of Greek salad.

MAKES 12 / READY IN 40 MINUTES

1 cup sliced pitted black olives

3 eggs

3½oz | 100g feta cheese, crumbled

½ cup freshly grated Parmesan cheese

1 onion, peeled and chopped

5 tbsp light olive oil

1¼ cups lowfat milk

generous 1¾ cups self-rising flour

1 tbsp freshly chopped thyme

salt and freshly ground black pepper

1 Preheat the oven to 400°F/200°C. Grease a 12-cup muffin pan or line with paper muffin liners.

2 Put the olives, eggs, feta cheese, half the Parmesan cheese, onion, oil, and milk into a large bowl and mix well together.

3 Stir in the flour and thyme and season with a pinch of salt and plenty of freshly ground black pepper. Mix until all the ingredients are well combined.

4 Spoon the muffin mixture into the prepared muffin pans and sprinkle over the remaining Parmesan cheese.

5 Bake for 25–30 minutes, or until well risen and firm.

Pesto muffins

Keep a jar of pesto in the refrigerator, then you can make these quickly if unexpected guests arrive. Great with roasted tomato soup or tomato and mozzarella salad. Add a handful of freshly chopped basil for a special occasion.

MAKES 9 / READY IN 40 MINUTES

⅓ cup pine nuts

1 garlic clove, peeled and crushed

5 tbsp light olive oil

2 eggs

6 tbsp pesto

½ cup grated Parmesan cheese

1 cup milk

1 cup self-rising flour

scant ½ cup whole-wheat flour

1 Preheat the oven to 400°F/200°C. Line 9 cups of a muffin pan with paper muffin liners.

2 Tip the pine nuts on a baking tray and place in the oven for 5 minutes, or until they become golden brown.

3 Put the garlic, olive oil, eggs, pesto, Parmesan, and milk into a large bowl. Stir everything together with a fork until well mixed.

4 Sift in the self-rising flour and whole-wheat flour, then add the toasted pine nuts. Gently work this into the wet mix.

5 Spoon the mixture into the paper muffin liners and bake for 15 minutes, or until well risen and firm.

Shrimp and peppadew muffins

Peppadews are one of those secret power-packed ingredients that's well worth seeking out. A South African favorite, they add a spicy yet piquant and sweet kick to dishes, yet are no way near as fierce as traditional chiles. They are sold pickled in jars, and you can choose from the hot or mild varieties.

MAKES 12 / READY IN 35 MINUTES

3¹⁄₂oz | 100g shrimp
2oz | 50g mild peppadews, chopped
1 scallion, trimmed and chopped
3¹⁄₂oz | 100g garlic and herb cheese
²⁄₃ cup sour cream
1 egg
5 tbsp light olive oil
²⁄₃ cup skim milk
1¹⁄₂ cups all-purpose flour
1 tbsp baking powder
1 tbsp superfine sugar
pinch of salt

1 Preheat the oven to 375°F/190°C. Line a 12-cup muffin pan with paper muffin liners.
2 Combine the shrimp, peppadew, scallios, cheese, and sour cream in a bowl. Add the egg, oil, and milk.
3 Stir in the flour, baking powder, sugar, and salt and mix until just combined.
4 Spoon the mixture into the prepared muffin liners. Bake for 20 minutes, or until well risen and firm.

Cheese, sage, and onion muffins

Use this basic recipe and vary the cheese to make the muffins taste different each time. Why not try one of the following: Emmental, Gruyère, Jarlsberg, Bavarian smoked, mature Cheddar, red Leicester, double Gloucester, Wensleydale, Stilton, or dolcelatte. This recipe is a great choice for diabetics.

MAKES 12 / READY IN 40 MINUTES

1 onion, peeled and chopped
4 tbsp light olive oil
1 egg
²⁄₃ cup lowfat milk
1¹⁄₂ cups self-rising flour
pinch of salt
2 tbsp poppy seeds
1 cup grated hard cheese
1 tbsp freshly chopped sage

1 Preheat the oven to 450°F/230°C. Line a 12-cup muffin tray with paper muffin liners.
2 Put the onion in a bowl with 1 tbsp of olive oil and microwave on high (850w) for 2¹⁄₂ minutes, or until tender. Alternatively, soften in a pan over gentle heat.
3 Pour the egg, milk, and 2 tbsp of olive oil into a pitcher and stir with a fork.
4 Sift the flour and salt into a bowl. Pour in the wet ingredients. Add the onion, half the poppy seeds, half the grated cheese, and the sage leaves. Mix together to make a stiff mixture.
5 Divide the mixture between the paper liners and sprinkle with the remaining cheese and poppy seeds. Drizzle the rest of the olive oil over the top.
6 Bake for 15 minutes, or until well risen and firm.

Healthy Selection

I'm always wary of store-bought products that are labeled "90% fat free." What it doesn't tell you on the packet, at first glance, is that although it's virtually fat free, it's laden with sugar. Then there's the sugar-free product, which is full of artificial sweeteners and fat. So what about the muffins included in this chapter? If you're following a sensible balanced diet and reserve one muffin for your treat of the day, these should be a guilt-free treat you can enjoy to eat. It may help to refer to the nutritional values on page 94. Freeze the rest of the batch to keep them out of temptation's way, and simply microwave them one at a time.

Blueberry and oat muffins

The oats and blueberries in these muffins are considered "super foods" by some nutritionists, capable of filling you up for longer and supplying longer-lasting energy.

MAKES 8 / READY IN 30 MINUTES

¾ cup whole-wheat flour

½ cup all-purpose flour

1 tbsp baking powder

½ tsp baking soda

¾ cup superfine sugar

1 cup rolled oats

1 egg

⅔ cup plain yogurt

¼ cup sunflower oil

½ tsp vanilla extract

½ cup blueberries

1 Preheat the oven to 400°F/200°C. Line a 12-cup muffin pan with 8 paper muffin liners.

2 Stir together flours, baking powder, and baking soda in a bowl. Stir in the sugar and most of the oats. Make a well in the center of the mixture.

3 Combine the egg, yogurt, oil, and vanilla extract in a pitcher. Add the egg mixture all at once to the flour mixture. Stir just until moistened (the batter should be lumpy). Fold the blueberries into the batter.

4 Spoon the batter into the prepared muffin liners, filling each three-quarters full.

5 Bake for 16–18 minutes, or until risen, firm yet springy, and a toothpick inserted into the center comes out clean. Cool or serve warm.

Lowfat berry and apple muffins

Not only are these muffins virtually fat-free, they're low in cholesterol and sugar too. If you're watching your weight, it's worth buying fructose because it's a natural product that's sweeter than sugar so you need less. It also has a lower glycemic index, so that you're less likely to experience the sugar highs and lows that make you feel hungry.

MAKES 12 / READY IN 35 MINUTES

1 cooking apple (8oz | 225g), peeled, cored, and chopped

4 tbsp fructose

1⅓ cups all-purpose flour

1½ tsp baking powder

¼ tsp baking soda

¾ tsp ground cinnamon

¼ tsp ground nutmeg

generous ¾ cup frozen berries (blackberries, raspberries, cherries, or a mixture)

1 cup bran

2 egg whites

1 cup lowfat plain yogurt

1 tbsp raw brown sugar

1 Preheat the oven to 400°F/200°C. Line a 12-cup muffin pan with paper muffin liners.

2 Put the cooking apple into a bowl with 1tbsp of fructose and 2tbsp of water. Microwave on high (850w) for 2 minutes, or until the apple is tender. (Alternatively, cook in a pan for a few minutes.) Whiz with a hand blender until smooth. Let cool.

3 In a large bowl, sift the flour, baking powder, baking soda, cinnamon, and nutmeg. Toss the berries in the rest of the fructose, then the bran, unwhisked egg whites, and yogurt.

4 Spoon the mixture into the paper muffin liners, then sprinkle with raw brown sugar and bake for 20 minutes, or until pale golden.

Lowfat yogurt and sour cherry

The perfect virtually fat-free recipe—no added butter or oil and egg-free too. This is a great recipe that you can vary slightly each time you make it. Try dried mango, papaya, apple, pear, or other dried red berries, or even chopped fresh fruit. Add a pinch of cinnamon, nutmeg, or allspice to vary the flavor even more.

MAKES 12 / READY IN 30 MINUTES

1½ cups all-purpose flour
2 tsp baking powder
1 tsp baking soda
¾ cup superfine sugar
scant ¼ cup sour cherries
⅔ cup lowfat plain yogurt
⅔ cup skim milk
1 tsp vanilla extract

1 Preheat the oven to 400°F/200°C. Line a 12-cup muffin pan with paper muffin liners.
2 Sift the flour, baking powder, and baking soda into a large bowl. Add the sugar and cherries and mix to combine.

3 Stir together the yogurt, milk, and vanilla extract, then pour into the dry ingredients and stir together until just combined.
4 Spoon the mixture into the paper liners. Bake for 18 minutes, or until well risen and firm yet springy.

Ricotta and spinach

Eat these flour and wheat-free muffins with a generous portion of green vegetables for a healthy, balanced meal. Super served warm or cold for a packed lunch or picnic as a great pastry-free alternative to quiche.

MAKES 12 / READY IN 35 MINUTES

1 tsp butter
⅓ cup pine nuts
8oz | 225g baby spinach leaves, washed
1½ cups ricotta
½ cup freshly grated Parmesan cheese
scant 1¼ cups sour cream
2 eggs
salt and freshly ground black pepper

1 Preheat the oven to 350°F/180°C. Grease a 12-cup muffin pan with butter.
2 Bake the pine nuts for 10 minutes, or until they are slightly browned.
3 Put the washed spinach into a bowl with 2tbsp cold water. Cover with plastic wrap, then pierce and microwave on high (850w) for 3 minutes, or until wilted. Alternatively, put the washed spinach in a pan and heat until just wilted. Tip into a strainer and squeeze out the excess water using a potato masher, then coarsely chop.

4 In a pitcher mix together the ricotta, Parmesan, sour cream, and eggs. Season with salt and freshly ground black pepper.
5 Stir in the spinach and toasted pine nuts.
6 Spoon into muffin pans and bake for 20 minutes, or until a toothpick inserted into the center comes out clean.

Cook's tip: Instead of ricotta, you can use a mixture of lowfat cream cheese and mild goat cheese.

Cinnamon English muffins

These muffins are virtually sugar free, yet are still delicious!

MAKES 10 / READY IN 1 HOUR
25 MINUTES

3 cups white bread flour

1 tsp ground cinnamon

1 tsp salt

¼oz envelope active dry yeast

1 tsp honey

1 cup milk

¼ cup butter

1 Sift the flour, cinnamon, and salt into a bowl. Microwave on medium (500w) for 1 minute to warm slightly (this simply helps the yeast to act more quickly, so don't worry if you don't have a microwave).

2 Add the yeast and honey to the flour.

3 Pour the milk into a pitcher. Add the butter and microwave on high (850w) for 1½ minutes to warm the milk and melt the butter. Alternatively, melt in a pan.

4 Stir all the liquid into the warm flour and beat well until smooth and elastic. Cover and prove in a warm place for 30 minutes, or until doubled in bulk.

5 Turn onto a well-floured board and knead, working in a little more flour if necessary to make the dough easier to shape. Round up the dough and roll into a thick sausage shape. Then, using a sharp knife, slice into 10 portions, each about 1¼ in | 3cm thick.

6 Use a plain cutter to help shape each one into a round with straight sides. Place, well spaced out, on a greased baking sheet. Cover with greased plastic wrap and put in a warm place to prove for 30–40 minutes, or until springy to the touch.

7 Heat a grill pan until really hot and grease lightly with butter. Lift the muffins carefully onto the hot grill pan and cook a few at a time over very low heat for 8–10 minutes, or until pale gold underneath. Turn over and cook the other side.

8 Wrap in a cloth and keep warm if cooking in batches. To serve, insert a knife in the side, then pull the top and bottom slightly apart and insert slivers of butter.

Cook's tip: To save time, make and prove the dough in a bread machine, then shape and bake conventionally. Try serving toasted and topped with mashed banana.

Whole-wheat yogurt and malted raisin

My favorite fat-free store-bought treat is malt loaf. I've added malt syrup to these muffins for a distinctive flavor—you'll find it sold in health food stores, as it is a good source of vitamin B. Virtually fat-free, these muffins make a guilt-free snack.

MAKES 12 / READY IN 30 MINUTES

⅔ cup all-purpose flour

½ tsp cinnamon

½ tsp allspice

2 tsp baking powder

1 tsp baking soda

pinch of salt

¾ cup whole-wheat flour

¾ cup superfine sugar

scant ¼ cup raisins

⅔ cup natural low-fat yogurt

1 tbsp malt syrup

⅔ cup skim milk

1 Preheat the oven to 400°F/200°C. Line a 12-cup muffin pan with paper muffin liners.

2 Sift the flour, cinnamon, allspice, baking powder, and baking soda into a large bowl with the salt. Add the whole-wheat flour, sugar, and raisins and mix.

3 Stir together the yogurt, malt syrup, and milk, then pour these into the dry ingredients and stir together until just combined.

4 Spoon the mixture into the paper liners. Bake for 18 minutes until risen, firm yet springy, and a toothpick inserted into the center comes out clean.

Butter-free chocolate and prune

What is the most common reaction to prunes? Err, no thanks. However, to my mind, the plump Californian ready-to-eat variety is an addictive snack. The other interesting discovery I made some years ago is that cooked and puréed prunes make a miraculous fat substitute. They keep the muffins moist and delicious, yet calorie-controlled and cholesterol free. When combined with cocoa, no one will guess your secret ingredient!

1 Preheat the oven to 375°F/190°C. Line 11 cups of a muffin pan with paper muffin liners.
2 Sift the all-purpose flour, cocoa, baking powder, baking soda, and salt into a bowl. Stir in the sugar.
3 Put the prunes into a food processor with 3 tbsp of water and whiz to make a smooth purée. Add an additional 1 cup of water, the egg whites, and vanilla extract. Whiz again to combine.

4 Pour the wet ingredients into the dry ingredients and stir until well blended.
5 Spoon the mixture into the prepared muffin liners and bake for 8–10 minutes, or until well risen and springy yet firm.
6 For the icing, sift the confectioners' sugar and cocoa together into a bowl, then stir in the milk until the icing is blended and smooth. Drizzle the icing over the cooled muffins to decorate.

MAKES 11 / READY IN 35 MINUTES
1 cup all-purpose flour
½ cup unsweetened cocoa
1½ tsp baking powder
¼ tsp baking soda
¼ tsp salt
1 cup superfine sugar
¾ cup pitted ready-to-eat prunes
3 large egg whites
1 tsp vanilla extract

For the chocolate icing:
1½ cups confectioners' sugar
1 tbsp unsweetened cocoa
1 tbsp skim milk

Tangy cranberry

These are a welcome treat, and not oversweet. The cranberries add a zingy fruitiness.

1 Heat the oven to 400°F/200°C. Line a 12-cup muffin pan with paper muffin liners.
2 Toss the cranberries in the confectioners' sugar to coat. Sift the flour and baking powder into a large bowl. Stir in the superfine sugar and cranberries.
3 In a large pitcher mix together the egg, milk, and butter. Add the wet ingredients to the dry ingredients and gently stir everything together until just combined.

4 Spoon into the muffin liners and bake for 15 minutes, until well risen and just firm.
5 Cool on a wire rack and dust with confectioners' sugar to serve.

Cook's tip: Cranberries are in season for only a short time. So stock up while they're in the stores and freeze for up to 6 months. Use straight from the freezer. Alternatively, use scant ⅔ cup of dried cranberries instead of the fresh; these are available all year. Omit the confectioners' sugar.

MAKES 12 / READY IN 35 MINUTES
⅔ cup fresh or frozen cranberries
¼ cup confectioners' sugar
1⅔ cups all-purpose flour
2 tsp baking powder
¾ cup superfine sugar
1 egg
1 cup milk
¼ cup unsalted butter, melted
confectioners' sugar, sifted for dusting

Egg and bacon treats

Basically flour-free, which makes them low in carbohydrates, these are quite unlike regular muffins in texture, but are still cooked in muffin pans for a defined shape. They would also be great for breakfast.

MAKES 9 / READY IN 35 MINUTES

1 tsp butter

7oz | 200g rindless trimmed smoked Canadian bacon, chopped

1 cup grated reduced fat sharp cheddar cheese

scant 1¼ cups sour cream

4 eggs

salt and freshly ground black pepper

1 Preheat the oven to 350°F/180°C. Grease 9 cups of a muffin pan.

2 Dry fry the bacon for a few minutes until it is browned and becoming crispy. (Alternatively, microwave on high (850w) for 4 minutes.)

3 In a pitcher use a fork to mix together the cheddar cheese, sour cream, and eggs. Season with salt and freshly ground black pepper. Stir in the bacon.

4 Spoon the mixture into the prepared muffin pans and bake for 20 minutes, or until firm.

Lowfat golden raisin and bran English muffins

Why not make and shape these when you have time to spare, cook some straightaway, and freeze the remainder unbaked?

MAKES 10 / READY IN 1 HOUR 25 MINUTES

1½ cups white bread flour

1 tsp salt

1½ cups stoneground whole-wheat flour

1 cup bran

⅓ cup golden raisins

¼oz envelope active dry yeast

1 tsp superfine sugar

1 cup milk

2 tbsp butter

1 Sift the white flour and salt into a bowl, then add the whole-wheat flour. Microwave on medium (500w) for 1 minute, to warm slightly. This simply helps the yeast to act more quickly, so don't worry if you don't have a microwave.

2 Add the bran, golden raisins, yeast, and sugar to the bowl.

3 Pour the milk into a pitcher. Add the butter and microwave on high (850w) for 1½ minutes to warm the milk and melt the butter. Alternatively, melt in a pan.

4 Stir all the liquid into the warm flour and beat well until smooth and elastic. Cover and prove in a warm place for 30 minutes, or until doubled in bulk.

5 Turn onto a well-floured board and knead, working in a little more flour if necessary to make the dough easier to shape. Round up the dough, then roll into

a thick sausage shape and, using a sharp knife, slice into 10 portions, each about 1¼in | 3cm thick.

6 Use a plain cutter to help shape each one into a round with straight sides. Place, well spaced out, on a greased baking sheet. Cover with greased plastic wrap and put in a warm place to prove for 30-40 minutes, or until springy to the touch.

7 Heat a grill pan until really hot and grease lightly with butter. Lift the muffins carefully onto the hot grill pan and cook a few at a time over very low heat for 15 minutes, or until pale gold underneath. Turn over and cook the other side.

8 Wrap in a cloth and keep warm if cooking in batches. To serve, insert a knife in the side, then pull the top and bottom slightly apart and insert slivers of butter.

Cook's tip: If the outer edges of the muffins begin to burn before the centers are cooked, wrap the muffins in nonstick parchment paper and bake at 400°F/200°C for 5 minutes. (Frozen muffins are best baked in this way after grilling.)

Special Diets

Just because these recipes have been designed for people with special dietary needs doesn't mean they're going to be less tasty. Healthy muffins with less fat and sugar are not a bad thing for any of us. If you're looking to expand your egg-free recipe repertoire, look for muffin recipes with just one egg, and replace it with 10 teaspoons milk. You'll be surprised how well it works. If you want to reduce your cholesterol, omit the butter and replace it with oil instead—use sunflower, vegetable, corn, or light olive oil. If you can't eat foods containing gluten, try using gluten-free flour instead of regular flour. Also look out for gluten free baking powder or make your own substitute using 1 part baking soda to 2 parts cream of tartar. For specific nutritional information on these recipes, please refer to pages 94–95.

Cornmeal scones

These are not quite as light as regular scones, but they still taste really good, especially when served warm from the oven.

1 Preheat the oven to 425°F/220°C. Place a baking sheet in the oven to heat up.
2 Put the cornmeal, gluten-free flour, baking powder, pinch of salt, and butter into a food processor. Whiz the mixture for 30 seconds, or until it turns into crumbs. Tip the mixture into a bowl.
3 Add the sugar and buttermilk to the bowl. Use a knife to mix everything together.

4 Knead the dough lightly on a surface covered with parchment paper to make smooth dough.
5 Roll out the dough to about 1in | 2.5cm thickness. Dip a 2½in | 6.5cm plain cutter in flour and use it to stamp out 9 rounds of dough.
6 Use a palette knife to lift the scones onto the preheated baking sheet. Brush the tops with milk and bake for 12–15 minutes, or until the scones are risen and pale golden. Split and serve with butter or cream cheese.

GLUTEN-FREE, EGG-FREE

MAKES 9 / READY IN 30 MINUTES
scant 1 cup cornmeal
1 cup gluten-free white flour
2 tsp gluten-free baking powder
pinch of salt
¼ cup butter, diced and chilled
2 tbsp superfine sugar
generous ¾ cup buttermilk
milk, to glaze

Carrot and pineapple muffins

Moist and irresistible, these muffins are egg and butter-free. For added fiber, you could use whole-wheat or granary flour.

1 Preheat the oven to 375°F/190°C. Line a 12-cup muffin pan with paper muffin liners.
2 Beat together the sugar, oil, and milk in a large bowl.
3 Sift in the flour, baking soda, and cinnamon. Stir to moisten, then add the vanilla extract, carrots, and pineapple.

4 Spoon the mixture into the prepared muffin liners and bake for 20 minutes, or until risen, firm yet springy, and a toothpick inserted into the center comes out clean.

Cook's tip: Add ⅔ cup chopped nuts with the carrots for a little more crunch.

EGG-FREE

MAKES 12 / READY IN 35 MINUTES
generous 1 cup superfine sugar
⅔ cup sunflower oil
⅔ cup lowfat milk
1½ cups self-rising flour
1 tsp baking soda
1 tsp cinnamon
1 tsp vanilla extract
7oz | 200g carrots, finely grated
7oz | 200g canned crushed pineapple, drained

Buckwheat and apple muffins

GLUTEN-FREE

Although buckwheat is actually a fruit seed related to rhubarb and sorrel, it behaves in a similar way to a cereal grain. For example, you can make buckwheat porridge. This makes it ideal for people who are sensitive to wheat or other grains that contain gluten. It adds an interesting texture to these muffins and gives a rich, dark brown color.

MAKES 12 / READY IN 35 MINUTES

⅔ cup honey

1 large egg

5 tbsp sunflower oil

5 tbsp skim milk

1 tsp vanilla extract

¾ cup buckwheat flour

generous ¾ cup gluten-free white flour

1 tsp cinnamon

2 tsp baking soda

2 eating apples, peeled, cored, and chopped

generous 1¼ cups raisins

1 cup walnuts, coarsely chopped

1 Heat the oven to 375°F/190°C. Line a 12-cup muffin pan with paper muffin liners.

2 Whisk together the honey, egg, oil, milk, and vanilla.

3 In a bowl, combine the buckwheat flour, gluten-free flour, cinnamon, and baking soda. Add the apples, raisins, and walnuts.

4 Stir the wet ingredients mixture into the apple mixture.

5 Spoon the mixture into the prepared muffin liners and bake for 15 minutes, or until pale golden, risen, and firm.

Gooseberry and almond muffins

GOOD FOR FIBER

Moist and fruity, these are lovely low-cholesterol muffins. When fresh gooseberries are not in season, use frozen. Cherries would work really well too, fresh when they're in season or drained, canned ones.

MAKES 12 / READY IN 35 MINUTES

generous ¾ cup superfine sugar

⅔ cup light olive oil

1 egg

scant ½ cup skim milk

1 tsp almond extract

1⅓ cups self-rising flour

1 tbsp baking powder

scant 1 cup ground almonds

1⅓ cups gooseberries, trimmed and halved

2 tbsp golden granulated sugar

2 tbsp slivered almonds

1 Heat the oven to 375°F/190°C. Line a 12-cup muffin pan with paper muffin liners.

2 Mix together the sugar, olive oil, egg, milk, and almond extract in a pitcher with a fork.

3 Sift the flour and baking powder into a bowl, then add the ground almonds and mix together.

4 Toss in the gooseberries and coat in the flour. Mix in the wet ingredients and stir everything together until just combined.

5 Spoon the mixture into the prepared muffin liners. Sprinkle the muffins with the granulated sugar and slivered almonds and bake for 15–20 minutes, or until pale golden, well risen, and firm.

Sweet potato muffins

The sweet potatoes in this mix make the muffins lovely and moist.

1 Pierce the sweet potato several times, then microwave on high (850w) for 6 minutes. Alternatively, boil the sweet potato in its skin for 15–20 minutes, or until tender. Peel away the skin, put the flesh into a bowl, then mash until smooth.
2 Heat the oven to 400°F/200°C. Line 9 cups of a muffin pan with paper muffin liners.

3 Mix together the oil, sugar, and eggs. Add the sweet potato, raisins, and walnuts and stir well.
4 Sift in the flour, baking powder, and ground allspice, and mix just enough to moisten. Do not overmix.
5 Spoon the mixture into the prepared muffin liners. Sprinkle with the spice sugar mix and bake for 20 minutes, or until pale golden, well risen, and firm.

MILK AND LACTOSE FREE

MAKES 9 / READY IN 35 MINUTES

8oz | 225g sweet potato, washed

5 tbsp sunflower oil

½ cup superfine sugar

2 eggs

scant ⅓ cup raisins

½ cup walnuts, chopped

scant 1¼ cups all-purpose flour

2 tsp baking powder

1 tsp ground allspice

3 tbsp golden granulated sugar mixed with ½ tsp ground allspice, for sprinkling

Bran, date, and prune muffins

These muffins are wholesome, satisfying, and high in fiber. Why not bake six, then keep the rest of the mixture in the refrigerator overnight—this enables the bran to swell and makes the muffins taste even more scrumptious.

1 Put the flour, baking soda, baking powder, allspice, sugar, bran, dates, and prunes into a bowl.
2 In a pitcher, combine the sunflower oil, buttermilk, and egg and mix until well blended.
3 Pour the wet ingredients into the dry, then mix until combined. Cover and chill some of the mixture overnight if you like.

4 Heat the oven to 375°F/190°C. Line a 12-cup muffin pan with paper muffin liners.
5 Spoon the mixture into the prepared muffin liners and bake for 20 minutes, or until pale golden, well risen and firm.

HIGH FIBER

MAKES 12 / READY IN 35 MINUTES

1 cup malt grain flour

2 tsp baking soda

2 tsp baking powder

½ tsp ground allspice

125g | 4oz dark brown sugar

1 cup oat bran

generous ½ cup dried pitted dates, chopped

generous ½ cup ready-to-eat pitted prunes, chopped

scant ½ cup sunflower oil

1¼ cups buttermilk

1 egg

Oatmeal and raspberry muffins

Oats and olive oil are good foods to eat if you are trying to reduce your cholesterol level. Using whole-wheat flour instead of all-purpose flour would be even more healthy, or use a mixture of the two.

LOW IN SATURATED FAT

MAKES 12 / READY IN 35 MINUTES

generous 1 cup rolled oats

1 cup skim milk

1 egg

1 cup superfine sugar

¼ cup light olive oil

1 cup all-purpose flour

2 tsp baking powder

½ tsp baking soda

⅔ cup raspberries

2 tbsp rolled oats, to sprinkle

1 Preheat the oven to 375°F/190°C. Line a 12-cup muffin pan with paper liners.

2 Put the oats into a bowl and add the milk.

3 In a pitcher mix together the egg, sugar, and olive oil to combine.

4 Sift the flour, baking powder and baking soda into a bowl, then gently toss in the raspberries.

5 Gently stir in the egg mixture, then the oats and milk.

6 Spoon the mixture into the muffin liners and sprinkle over the rolled oats. Bake for 15-20 minutes, or until well risen and firm.

Cook's tip: Add ½ tsp of cinnamon for added flavor. It's fine to use raspberries straight from the freezer, as this will help them to keep their shape rather than becoming squashed during mixing. Chopped dried apples, apricots, blueberries, cherries, dates, pears, raisins, or golden raisins also taste good.

Lactose-free zucchini muffins

These have an interesting and mildly sweet flavor, so give them a try. We're all used to carrot cake, so why not zucchini?

LACTOSE-FREE

MAKES 12 / READY IN 35 MINUTES

3 eggs

scant ½ cup sunflower oil

5 tbsp water

1¼ cups superfine sugar

12oz | 350g zucchini, grated

2 tsp baking powder

1 tsp ground cinnamon

1 tsp nutmeg

1½ cups all-purpose flour

¾ cup raisins

1 Preheat the oven to 375°F/190°C. Line a 12-cup muffin pan with paper muffin liners.

2 Mix together the eggs, sunflower oil, water, sugar, and zucchini in a large bowl.

3 Add the baking powder, cinnamon, nutmeg, all-purpose flour, and raisins and blend until just mixed.

4 Spoon the mixture into the prepared muffin liners and bake for 15-20 minutes, or until pale golden, well risen, and firm yet springy.

Cook's tip: For chocolate muffins, replace 4 tbsp of the all-purpose flour with unsweetened cocoa. (These taste even better.)

Herb Popovers

LOW-CARB

These are similar to English Yorkshire puddings, but the main difference is that you can start cooking these in a cold oven, unlike the English version which always needs a sizzling hot oven to start.

MAKES 6 KING-SIZE MUFFINS / READY IN 30-40 MINUTES

⅔ cup all-purpose flour

¼ tsp salt

2 tbsp freshly chopped herbs (such as chives, parsley, thyme, sage, basil, or a mixture)

3 eggs

1 cup lowfat milk

1 Put the flour, salt, and herbs into a bowl. Butter 6 cups of a king-size muffin pan.

2 In a pitcher mix the eggs and milk together very well with a fork.

3 Pour the wet ingredients into the dry and mix together with a fork until lump-free. Pour the batter into the buttered muffin pan.

4 Turn on the oven to 425°F/220°C. Put the popovers into a cold oven.

5 Cook for 25-30 minutes. For drier popovers, pierce each one with a knife and cook for 5 more minutes.

Sugar-free double-corn muffins

SUGAR-FREE

These muffins are ideal for diabetics and make a perfect replacement for bread. They're best eaten within two days of making. Freeze extras and defrost in the microwave until they are just warm to serve.

MAKES 9 / READY IN 35 MINUTES

⅔ cup cornmeal

generous ¾ cup all-purpose flour

1 tbsp baking powder

¼ tsp salt

2 cups corn

1 egg, lightly beaten

5 tbsp sunflower oil

scant 1¼ cups buttermilk

1 Preheat the oven to 400°C/200°F. Line 9 cups of a muffin pan with paper muffin liners.

2 Put the cornmeal, flour, baking powder, and salt into a mixing bowl.

3 Add the corn, egg, oil, and buttermilk, stirring well.

4 Spoon the mixture into the prepared muffin liners and bake for 20 minutes, or until pale golden, well risen, and firm.

Scones

I was taught how to make English scones at school, and I think that's what may have put me off making them for ages. My memories are of rock-hard, tasteless mini-bricks. Maybe I didn't eat them the day they were made, or maybe I was too scared to add enough liquid to the dough to make it pliable. Well, all these recipes are foolproof. Homemade scones are soft, light, and especially gorgeous eaten within a few hours of baking. They're the perfect accompaniment to a steaming cup of tea. Freezing the unbaked dough is a great option—just cook from the freezer for an extra 3 minutes.

English afternoon tea scones

These traditional scones are divine served with the updated alternative to clotted cream—mascarpone cream and jelly.

MAKES 8 / READY IN 30 MINUTES

1½ cups self-rising flour
1 tsp baking powder
pinch of salt
2 tbsp superfine sugar
¼ cup butter, cubed
1 egg, lightly beaten
5 tbsp milk, plus a little extra to glaze

For the filling:
scant ½ cup mascarpone cheese
4 tbsp Greek-style yogurt
2 tbsp superfine sugar
½ tsp vanilla extract
½ cup strawberry jelly

1 Preheat the oven to 450°F/230°C. Place an ungreased baking sheet in the oven to heat up.

2 Sift the flour, baking powder, and salt together into a bowl and add the sugar.

3 Add the butter and rub together with your fingertips to make crumbs.

4 Pour in the egg and milk and bring the mixture together with your hands to make a soft manageable dough. Roll out dough on a lightly floured surface until it is ¾in | 2cm thick. Use a 2in | 5cm plain cutter to stamp out 8 rounds.

5 Use a palette knife to lift the scones onto the preheated baking sheet. Brush the tops with milk.

6 Bake for 8–10 minutes, or until well risen, firm, and golden. Cool on a wire rack.

7 Mix together the mascarpone, Greek-style yogurt, sugar, and vanilla until well combined. Split scones in half and serve with a dollop of mascarpone and jelly.

Cook's tip: You can still make these scones even if you have run out of eggs by using ⅔ cup milk or even a mixture of water and milk. They'll be slightly less rich, but tasty all the same.

Malt grain scones

I find that whole-wheat goodies become addictive; the more you eat, the more you enjoy them. So here's a satisfying treat with an interesting texture. It's tasty cut in half and spread with butter and jelly.

MAKES 8 / READY IN 30 MINUTES

1½ cups malt or multi-grain flour

1 tbsp baking powder

pinch of salt

1 tbsp superfine sugar

¼ cup butter, cubed

⅔ cup skim milk, plus a little extra to glaze

1 Preheat the oven to 450°F/230°C. Place an ungreased baking sheet in the oven to heat up.

2 Tip the flour, baking powder, and salt into a bowl and add the sugar.

3 Add the butter and rub together with your fingertips to make crumbs.

4 Pour in the milk and bring the mixture together with your hands to make a soft, manageable dough. Roll out dough on a lightly floured surface until it is ¾in | 2cm thick. Use a 2in | 5cm plain cutter to stamp out 8 rounds.

5 Use a palette knife to lift the scones onto the preheated baking sheet. Brush the tops with milk.

6 Bake for 8–10 minutes, or until well risen, firm, and golden.

Sunflower seed and honey scones

Sunflower seeds are a brilliant source of vitamin E, and folic acid, other B vitamins, and minerals including copper and magnesium. The seeds add an interesting crunchiness to the scones.

MAKES 8 / READY IN 30 MINUTES

generous ¾ cup white self-rising flour

pinch of salt

1 tsp baking powder

scant ⅔ cup whole-wheat self-rising flour

½ cup sunflower seeds

¼ cup butter, cubed

1 egg, lightly beaten

5 tbsp milk, plus a little extra to glaze

2 tbsp honey

1 Preheat the oven to 450°F/230°C. Place an ungreased baking sheet in the oven to heat up.

2 Sift the self-rising flour, salt, and baking powder together into a bowl, then add the whole-wheat flour and half of the seeds.

3 Add the butter and rub together with your fingertips to make crumbs.

4 Pour in the egg, milk, and honey and bring the mixture together with your hands to make it a soft, manageable dough. Roll out dough on a lightly floured surface until it is ¾in | 2cm thick. Use a 2in | 5cm fluted cutter to stamp out 8 rounds.

5 Use a palette knife to lift the scones onto the preheated baking sheet. Brush the tops with milk and sprinkle with the rest of the sunflower seeds.

6 Bake for 8–10 minutes, or until well risen, firm, and golden. Cool on a wire rack, then serve split and buttered, with extra thick honey.

Cheddar and thyme scones

Serve these scones with cheese, chutney, and celery stalks at lunchtime to make a change from bread.

1 Preheat the oven to 425°F/220°C. Place an ungreased baking sheet in the oven to heat up.
2 Sift the flour, salt, and baking powder into a bowl and rub in the butter, until the mixture forms into crumbs.
3 Stir in half the cheese. Strip the thyme leaves off the stalks and add the leaves along with the mustard and enough milk to give a fairly soft dough.

4 Roll out dough on a lightly floured surface until it is ¾in | 2cm thick. Use a 2in | 5cm plain cutter to stamp out 8 rounds.
5 Use a palette knife to lift the scones onto the baking sheet. Brush the tops with milk and sprinkle with the rest of the cheese.
6 Bake for 8–10 minutes, or until well risen, firm, and golden.

MAKES 8 / READY IN 30 MINUTES

1½ cups self-rising flour
pinch of salt
1 tsp baking powder
3 tbsp butter
¾ cup grated sharp cheddar cheese
2 thyme sprigs
1 tsp whole-grain mustard
⅔ cup milk, plus a little extra to glaze

Carrot and raisin scones

This is an interesting combination that's not oversweet. I recommend them spread with cream cheese.

1 Preheat the oven to 425°F/220°C. Place an ungreased baking sheet in the oven to heat up.
2 Put the flour, baking powder, salt, and butter in a food processor. Whiz the mixture for 30 seconds, or until the mixture turns into crumbs. Tip the mixture into a bowl.
3 Add the sugar, raisins, carrots, and buttermilk. Use a knife to mix everything together.

4 Knead the dough lightly on a floured surface to make a smooth dough. Roll out the dough to a thickness of about 1in | 2.5cm.
5 Dip a 2½in | 6.5cm plain cutter in some flour, then use it to stamp out 8 rounds of dough.
6 Use a palette knife to lift the scones onto the preheated baking sheet. Brush the tops with milk and bake for 12–15 minutes, or until the scones are risen and pale golden.

MAKES 8 / READY IN 30 MINUTES

1⅔ cups self-rising flour, sifted
1 tsp baking powder
pinch of salt
¼ cup butter, diced and chilled
2 tbsp superfine sugar
scant ⅓ cup raisins
3oz | 75g carrots, grated
1 cup buttermilk
milk, to glaze

Whole-wheat scone round

Although these are called whole-wheat scones, they do contain some all-purpose flour to guarantee that they are light. Using brown flour on its own would make the texture of the scone too dense.

SERVES 6 / READY IN 30 MINUTES

⅓ cup all-purpose flour

pinch of salt

1 tbsp baking powder

scant 1¼ cups whole-wheat flour

¼ cup superfine sugar

¼ cup butter, cubed

⅔ cup milk

1 Preheat the oven to 425°F/220°C. Place an ungreased baking sheet in the oven to heat up.
2 Sift the white flour, salt, and baking powder together into a bowl. Tip in the whole-wheat flour and sugar.
3 Add the butter and rub together with your fingertips to make crumbs.
4 Pour in the milk and bring the mixture together with your hands to make it a soft, manageable dough.

5 Shape into a flat 6in | 15cm round. Mark into 6 triangular slices using the back of floured knife.
6 Put the scone onto the preheated baking sheet and bake at once for 15 minutes, or until pale golden. To test if it is cooked, tap the base with your knuckle—it should sound hollow.

Vanilla and buttermilk scones

The more expensive your vanilla flavoring, the more pungent the flavor will be. Artificial vanilla flavoring is best avoided. Splurge on the real thing—vanilla extract—and you'll appreciate its distinctive flavor. Yet more indulgent is vanilla bean paste. It is a fantastic ingredient; expensive, but a little goes a long way. It's thicker than vanilla extract and contains millions of the tiny vanilla seeds you find when you split a vanilla bean.

MAKES 8 / READY IN 30 MINUTES

1⅔ cups self-rising flour, sifted

1 tsp baking powder

pinch of salt

¼ cup butter, diced and chilled

2 tbsp superfine sugar

1 cup buttermilk

1 tsp vanilla bean paste or vanilla extract

milk, to glaze

1 Preheat the oven to 425°F/220°C. Place an ungreased baking sheet in the oven to heat up.
2 Tip the flour, baking powder, salt, and butter in a food processor. Whiz the mixture for 30 seconds, or until the mixture turns into crumbs. Tip the mixture into a bowl.
3 Add the sugar, buttermilk, and vanilla bean paste or extract. Use a knife to mix everything together.

4 Knead the dough lightly on a floured surface to make a smooth dough. Roll out the dough to a thickness of about 1in | 2.5cm.
5 Dip a 2½in | 6.5cm plain cutter in some flour, then use it to stamp out 8 rounds of dough.
6 Use a palette knife to lift the scones onto the preheated baking sheet. Brush the tops with milk and bake for 12–15 minutes, or until the scones are risen and pale golden. Split and serve with jelly.

Buttermilk drop scones

These are very similar to pancakes but in Ireland they are made using buttermilk and are called drop scones. So speedy to make— perfect for a comforting dessert or afternoon treat.

1 Sift the flour, baking powder, and salt into a bowl. Make a well in the center.
2 Mix together the eggs, buttermilk, and 3 tbsp cold water, then pour the wet ingredients into the dry and whisk everything together to make a smooth batter.
3 Heat the oil in a large, heavy-bottom pan. Add 3 separate ladlefuls of the mixture to the hot pan. Cook for 2–3 minutes until the bases are firm, then use a spatula to turn the pancakes over. Cook for an additional 2–3 minutes, or until the pancakes are spongy and cooked through.

4 Put the blueberries and sugar into a pan with scant ½ cup water. Bring to a boil and simmer for a few minutes. Mix the arrowroot with 1 tbsp cold water to make a smooth paste, then add to the pan. Stir over the heat until thickened and smooth.
5 Serve 2–3 pancakes layered up and drizzled with the blueberries in syrup.

Cooks tip: These taste just as good drizzled with maple syrup and sliced bananas. Or try them sprinkled with superfine sugar and a squeeze of lemon.

MAKES 6 / READY IN 15 MINUTES

scant 1¼ cups all-purpose flour
½ tsp baking powder
pinch of salt
3 large eggs
⅔ cup buttermilk
2 tbsp sunflower oil

To serve:
1 cup blueberries
¼ cup superfine sugar
1 tsp arrowroot

Blueberry and cinnamon scones

Dried blueberries make a welcome change from more common dried fruit, such as golden raisins, and the hint of cinnamon is lovely. Split and spread with a little butter is all you need.

MAKES 8 / READY IN 30 MINUTES

1⅔ cups self-rising flour, sifted
1 tsp baking powder
½ tsp cinnamon
pinch of salt
¼ cup butter, diced and chilled
2 tbsp superfine sugar
1 cup buttermilk
⅓ cup dried blueberries
milk to glaze

1 Preheat the oven to 425°F/220°C. Place an ungreased baking sheet in the oven to heat up.
2 Tip the flour, baking powder, cinnamon, salt, and butter in a food processor. Whiz the mixture for 30 seconds until it turns into crumbs. Tip the mixture into a bowl.
3 Add the sugar, buttermilk, and blueberries. Use a knife to mix everything together.

4 Knead the dough lightly on a floured surface to make a smooth dough. Roll out to a thickness of about 2.5cm | 1 in.
5 Dip a 2½in | 6.5cm plain cutter in some flour, then use it to stamp out 8 rounds of dough.
6 Use a palette knife to lift the scones onto the preheated baking sheet. Brush the tops with milk and bake for 12–15 minutes, or until the scones are risen and pale golden.

Cranberry and walnut scones

These scones are a great combination of ingredients. They are at their best when split and served with blueberry jelly.

MAKES 8 / READY IN 30 MINUTES

50g | 2oz walnuts
1⅔ cups self-rising flour, sifted
scant ⅓ cup self-rising whole-wheat flour
1 tsp baking powder
pinch of salt
¼ cup butter, diced and chilled
2 tbsp superfine sugar
⅓ cup dried cranberries
1 cup buttermilk
milk, to glaze

1 Preheat the oven to 425°F/220°C. Place an ungreased baking sheet in the oven to heat up.
2 Put the walnuts into a processor and whiz until finely ground.
3 Add the flours, baking powder, salt, and butter to the food processor. Whiz the mixture for 30 seconds, or until it turns into crumbs. Tip the mixture into a bowl.
4 Add the sugar, cranberries, and buttermilk. Use a knife to mix everything together.

5 Knead the dough lightly on a floured surface to make a smooth dough. Roll out to a thickness of about 1in | 2.5cm.
6 Dip a 2½in | 6.5cm plain cutter in some flour, then use it to stamp out 8 rounds of dough.
7 Use a palette knife to lift the scones onto the preheated baking sheet. Brush the tops with milk and bake for 12–15 minutes, or until the scones are risen and pale golden. Split and serve with jelly.

Time to Indulge

I've a confession to make. The only reason I really started cooking was because I'm greedy. If I had a chocolate craving, the fastest and most efficient way of getting that satisfying hit was to whip something up in the kitchen. If I was feeling lazy, I may have munched on raisins or a banana, or tried coffee with frothy milk and an extra-large sprinkling of chocolate, but by the time I'd waded through all those nibbles, I hadn't fully satisfied the craving and I'd still consumed a fair few calories. So, for those times when only the biggest and best will do, here are ten totally wicked muffins.

Preserved ginger muffins

I adore ginger—the stronger the flavor, the better it is for me. Look out for crystallized ginger that has a fantastically powerful ginger hit—it's great to use for decorating cakes and muffins. Preserved ginger in syrup never fails to please, either. These muffins will keep for up to a week, stored in a cool place in an airtight container.

1 Heat the oven to 350°F/180°C. Line a 6-cup king-size muffin pan with paper muffin liners.
2 Put the butter, sugar, and dark molasses into a pitcher and microwave on high (850w) for 2 minutes, or until everything has melted together. Alternatively, heat gently in a pan, then pour into a pitcher.
3 Add the milk and Southern Comfort, if using, to the pitcher and mix together. Stir in the egg.
4 Sift the flour, spices, and baking soda into a large mixing bowl. Stir in the preserved ginger and apricots to coat.

5 Make a well in the center and pour in the wet ingredients. Stir gently until everything is combined.
6 Spoon the mixture into the muffin liners and bake for 20–25 minutes, or until well risen and firm.

Cook's tip: Once opened, brown sugar can quickly go hard. Make it spoonable again by microwaving on defrost (150w) for 30 seconds per about 225g | 8oz.

MAKES 6 KING-SIZE MUFFINS / READY IN 40 MINUTES

scant ½ cup butter
½ cup dark brown sugar
3 tbsp dark molasses
scant ½ cup skim milk
2 tbsp Southern Comfort, optional
1 large egg
1 cup all-purpose flour
1 tbsp ground ginger
2 tsp ground cinnamon
1 tsp baking soda
6 pieces preserved ginger, drained from syrup and coarsely chopped
½ cup dried apricots, chopped

Strawberries and cream

If you have bought strawberries that have gone mushy sooner than expected, put them to good use in these divine dessert muffins. Serve them topped with whole strawberries and fresh vanilla cream.

1 Heat the oven to 400°F/200°C. Line a 6-cup king-size muffin pan with paper muffin liners.
2 Sift the flour and baking powder into a bowl. Add the sugar and gently stir in the strawberries, to coat.
3 In a pitcher mix the eggs, oil, milk, and vanilla extract. Beat until well blended.
4 Add the egg mixture to the flour mixture and stir for just 10–15 strokes to combine.

5 Spoon the mixture into the paper liners. Bake for 20 minutes, or until well risen and firm. Cool on a wire rack.
6 Whip the cream with the sugar and vanilla extract until just standing in soft peaks. Put a dollop of cream on top of each muffin and serve with a fresh strawberry.

MAKES 6 KING-SIZE MUFFINS / READY IN 30 MINUTES

2 cups all-purpose flour
2 tsp baking powder
generous ¾ cup superfine sugar
generous ¾ cup strawberries, chopped
3 eggs
5 tbsp sunflower oil
scant ½ cup skim milk
1 tsp vanilla extract

To serve:
⅔ cup heavy cream
1 tbsp superfine sugar
½ tsp vanilla extract
6 whole strawberries

Mixed nut muffins

These are great eaten straight from the oven, but also good enjoyed one or two days later when the moisture in the sugar softens the muffins.

MAKES 4 KING-SIZE MUFFINS / READY IN 35 MINUTES

scant ½ cup whole-wheat flour

scant 1¼ cups all-purpose flour

scant ½ cup dark brown sugar

1 tbsp baking powder

¼ tsp baking soda

1 cup mixed nuts, such as pecans, macadamias, and hazelnuts, chopped

4 tbsp dark corn syrup

5 tbsp sunflower oil

⅔ cup skim milk

1 Heat the oven to 375°F/190°C. Line 4 cups of a king-size muffin pan with paper muffin liners.
2 Put the whole-wheat flour, all-purpose flour, sugar, baking powder, baking soda, and most of the nuts in a large bowl and mix well.
3 Pour ¼ cup boiling water into a pitcher. Dip a tablespoon (the measuring spoon type) into the hot water and use to measure out the dark corn syrup, then add to the water with the oil and milk.
4 Quickly mix the wet ingredients into the dry and spoon the mixture into the muffin liners. Sprinkle over the reserved nuts.
5 Bake for about 20–25 minutes, or until risen, just firm to the touch, and a toothpick inserted into the center comes out clean.

Coconut, carrot, pecan, and pineapple muffins

These are the kind of muffins that would be labeled "healthy" in the stores, just because they've got carrots in the ingredients list. This is really the indulgent version of a good-for-you muffin, but each one contains a fruit and vegetable so they're certainly not all bad.

MAKES 6 KING-SIZE MUFFINS / READY IN 60 MINUTES

1½ cups all-purpose flour

1 tsp ground cinnamon

1 tsp allspice

1 tbsp baking powder

½ tsp salt

scant 1¼ cups superfine sugar

generous ½ cup shredded sweetened coconut

9oz | 250g carrots, peeled and grated

1 apple, peeled, cored, and grated

scant ⅔ cup raisins

¾ cup pecans or walnuts, coarsely chopped

scant 1 cup crushed pineapple, drained from can

2 eggs

⅔ cup vegetable oil

⅔ cup sour cream

1 tsp vanilla extract

1 Heat the oven to 375°F/190°C. Line a 6-cup king-size muffin pan with paper muffin liners.
2 Sift together the flour, cinnamon, allspice, baking powder, and salt. Stir in the sugar, coconut, carrot, apple, raisins, nuts, and pineapple.
3 In a pitcher, whisk together the eggs, oil, sour cream, and vanilla extract. Pour into the bowl with the dry ingredients and stir together until just combined.
4 Spoon the batter into the paper liners, filling them almost to the top. Bake for 25–30 minutes, until risen, firm, and springy, or until a toothpick inserted into the center comes out clean.
5 Cool the muffins in the pan for about 10 minutes, then turn out onto a wire rack to cool completely. Store in an airtight container. Best eaten the next day, if you can wait.

Sticky toffee and date muffins

As these muffins come with a sticky toffee sauce, serve them warm as a gorgeous dessert.

MAKES 8 KING-SIZE MUFFINS / READY IN 40 MINUTES

1 tsp butter, for greasing

1½ cups pitted dates, coarsely chopped

1 tsp baking soda

¼ cup butter

1½ cups self-rising flour, sieved

2 tsp baking powder

scant 1 cup dark brown sugar

2 large eggs, lightly beaten

For the toffee sauce:

¼ cup butter

generous ⅓ cup dark brown sugar

scant ⅔ cup heavy cream

4 tbsp Greek yogurt

1 Heat the oven to 350°F/180°C. Grease 8 cups in a king-size muffin pan.

2 Put the dates into a large pitcher and add the baking soda and the butter. Pour over 1 cup boiling water and let stand for a few minutes to cool slightly. Then whiz to a smooth purée in a processor.

3 Sift the flour and baking powder into a large bowl, then add the sugar, eggs, and date purée and stir until just combined.

4 Spoon into the prepared muffin pans and bake for 25 minutes, or until risen, firm, and springy.

5 Meanwhile, for the sauce, put the butter, sugar, and scant ½ cup of the cream into a large pitcher. Microwave on high (850w) for 2 minutes, then stir and cook for another 2 minutes, or until the sauce is melted and smooth. Alternatively, heat in a pan and stir until melted.

6 Whip the remaining cream and mix with the yogurt. Serve the muffins drizzled with the warm toffee sauce and a dollop of cream mixture.

Vanilla bean muffins

Real vanilla beans are the fermented and dried seedpods of an orchid native to Mexico. They are expensive but the flavor is intense. When split in half, you can scrape out the hundreds of tiny vanilla seeds hidden within. However, look out for vanilla bean paste in the gourmet section of your supermarket—it's the perfect connoisseur's cheat. Alternatively, use real vanilla extract, but although it has a great authentic flavor, you'll have none of the characteristic seeds.

MAKES 6 KING-SIZE MUFFINS / READY IN 30 MINUTES

1½ cups all-purpose flour

¾ cup superfine sugar

1 tbsp baking powder

¼ tsp baking soda

1 egg, beaten

1 cup thick vanilla yogurt

1½ tbsp vanilla extract

scant ½ cup butter, melted

2 tbsp vanilla or granulated sugar

1 Heat the oven to 375°F/190°C. Line 6 cups of a king-size muffin pan with paper muffin liners.

2 In a large bowl, combine the flour, sugar, baking powder, and baking soda.

3 In a pitcher, mix the egg, yogurt, and vanilla together well.

4 Pour the wet ingredients over dry, then add the melted butter and stir just to blend (just a few strokes, do not over mix).

5 Spoon the batter evenly into the prepared muffin liners. Sprinkle the tops with vanilla or granulated sugar, if using, and bake for 25 minutes.

Dark chocolate truffle muffins

Every chocoholic's fantasy, these are wicked served with ice cream. Use bitter chocolate with at least 50 percent cocoa solids.

MAKES 12 / READY IN 40 MINUTES

1 tsp butter, for greasing

7oz | 200g dark chocolate (50% cocoa solids or more), broken into squares

scant 1 cup unsalted butter, cubed

1⅓ cups self-rising flour

¼ tsp baking powder

2 tbsp cocoa powder

¾ cup superfine sugar

⅔ cup milk

3 eggs

1 large chocolate caramel bar, cut into 12 pieces

For the truffle sauce:

3½oz | 100g each of dark and milk chocolate, broken into squares

1 tbsp dark corn syrup

2 tbsp milk or cream

1 Heat the oven to 350°F/180°C. Grease a 12-cup muffin pan.
2 Put the chocolate and butter in a heatproof bowl. Microwave on medium (500w) for 2 minutes. Stir and microwave for 2 more minutes, or until smooth.
3 In a large bowl, stir together the flour, baking powder, cocoa, and sugar.
4 In a pitcher, lightly mix together the milk and eggs with a fork, then stir into the dry ingredients, along with the melted chocolate. Mix to combine.
5 Put a spoonful of mixture into the base of each muffin cup and top with a slice of the chocolate caramel bar. Top with the remaining muffin mixture.
6 Bake for 18–20 minutes, or until risen.
7 For the truffle sauce, heat the chocolate with the dark corn syrup and milk or cream. Microwave on medium (500w) for 2 minutes. Stir and cook for 1 more minute, until the chocolate is melted and smooth.
8 Serve the muffins topped with caramel slices and drizzled with truffle sauce.

Tiramisu muffins

What a wonderful combination—chocolate, coffee, and an alcoholic coffee mascarpone topping.

MAKES 12 / READY IN 40 MINUTES

2½ cups self-rising flour

½ tsp baking soda

2 tbsp unsweetened cocoa

¾ cup dark brown sugar

3½oz | 100g dark chocolate, coarsely grated

2oz | 50g white chocolate, coarsely grated

1 large egg

scant ½ cup sunflower oil

generous ¾ cup strong black coffee, cooled

generous ¾ cup skim milk

For the topping:

3 tbsp coffee liqueur, optional

generous 1 cup mascarpone cheese

2 tbsp milk

4 tbsp unrefined confectioners' sugar

1 tbsp cocoa, sifted

1 Heat the oven to 400°F/200°C. Line a 12-cup muffin pan with paper muffin liners.
2 Sift the flour, baking soda, and cocoa into a large bowl. Stir in the sugar and the dark and white chocolate.
3 In a large pitcher mix together the egg, sunflower oil, cooled black coffee, and milk.
4 Pour the wet ingredients into the dry and stir together lightly until just combined. Do not overmix.
5 Spoon the mixture into the paper liners and bake for 20 minutes, or until the muffins are well risen, firm yet springy, and a toothpick inserted into the center comes out clean.
6 Pierce several times with a toothpick and drizzle over the coffee liqueur, if using.
7 Mix together the mascarpone, milk, and sifted confectioners' sugar until smooth. Use a palette knife to spread over the cooled muffins. Dust with cocoa to finish.

Luxury lemon muffins

These lemon muffins taste fantastic straight from the oven. Make the limoncello syrup as an additional treat, but they taste really good without it too!

1 Heat the oven to 350°F/180°C. Line 8 cups of a king-size muffin pan with paper muffin liners.

2 Sift the flour into a large bowl and add the sugar.

3 In a separate bowl, mix together the yogurt, milk, egg, grated lemon zest, and lemon juice.

4 Melt the butter in the microwave on high (850w) for 30 seconds, or melt in a pan. Add all the wet ingredients to the dry and gently stir.

5 Spoon the mixture into the prepared muffin pans. Bake for 20 minutes, until the muffins are well risen, firm, and a toothpick inserted into the center comes out clean.

6 Meanwhile, make the lemon syrup, if you wish to. Put the shredded lemon zest and juice into a pan with the sugar. Heat gently, stirring to dissolve the sugar. Simmer for 5 minutes, then add the limoncello, if using.

7 Pour over a little warm syrup and zest while the muffins are warm.

MAKES 8 KING-SIZE MUFFINS / READY IN 30 MINUTES

2 cups self-rising flour

scant 1 cup superfine sugar

⅔ cup plain yogurt

6 tbsp skim milk

1 large egg

finely grated zest and juice of 3 unwaxed lemons

scant ½ cup unsalted butter

For the lemon syrup (optional):

peeled and finely shredded zest and juice of 2 unwaxed lemons

generous ½ cup superfine sugar

2 tbsp limoncello (Italian lemon liqueur) (optional)

Mini golden Victoria sandwiches

There's something good about an old-fashioned Victoria sandwich cake, perhaps because you get oodles of extra sweetness in the filling in what may otherwise be a plain cake. These modern mini sandwich cakes are packed with caramelly flavors, thanks to the variety of sugars this recipe uses.

1 Heat the oven to 375°F/190°C. Grease a 12-cup muffin pan with butter.

2 Sift the flour and baking powder into a bowl, then add both the sugars.

3 In a pitcher, mix together the melted butter, vanilla extract, and milk, then add the eggs and mix with a fork to combine.

4 Pour the wet ingredients into the dry and stir together until thoroughly combined.

5 Spoon into the greased muffin pan and bake for 15 minutes, or until risen, firm yet

springy, and a toothpick inserted into the center comes out clean.

6 Cool the muffins on a wire rack and cut each one in half horizontally.

7 Put the mascarpone cheese into a bowl with the yogurt and stir until smooth. Stir in the sugar and vanilla extract. Sandwich the two muffin halves together with a dollop of jelly and a smothering of the mascarpone cheese. Dust the tops with sifted confectioners' sugar.

MAKES 12 / READY IN 60 MINUTES

1 tsp butter

1½ cups self-rising flour

1 tsp baking powder

generous ½ cup dark brown sugar

½ cup superfine sugar

¾ cup butter, melted

2 tsp vanilla extract

5 tbsp skim milk

3 large eggs

For the filling:

scant 1 cup mascarpone cheese

⅔ cup Greek-style yogurt

2 tbsp superfine sugar

½ tsp vanilla extract

12 tsp strawberry jelly

2 tbsp unrefined confectioners' sugar

Fit for a Celebration

So many cakes are all about presentation and nothing about flavor. The worst offenders are store-bought birthday cakes. Does anybody actually enjoy eating a slice? In my experience, children pick off the decorations and leave the rest. Big cakes can be daunting to make and sometimes the results are disappointing, so here I've used traditional cake recipes and adapted them to fit into muffin cups. They taste divine, look impressive, and you can happily serve leftovers without them looking sad. Bake several batches and freeze ahead if you're catering for a crowd. Show them off in style by arranging them carefully on a series of thin cake boards in decreasing sizes, stacked up with cake pillars. Finish off with candles for a really memorable display!

Lavender and lemon birthday muffins

A hint of fresh lavender gives an old-fashioned, interesting fragrance to what would otherwise be a plain lemon muffin (though still good if lavender's not in season). It also makes a pretty decoration that's original yet hassle-free.

MAKES 6 KING-SIZE MUFFINS / READY IN 30 MINUTES

1 tsp butter

5 heads of fresh lavender

¾ cup superfine sugar

1½ cups self-rising flour

finely grated zest and juice of 2 unwaxed lemons

2 eggs

⅔ cup sunflower oil

generous ¾ cup sour cream

For the icing:

¾ cup confectioners' sugar

2–3 tbsp lemon juice

3 heads of fresh lavender

1 Heat the oven to 375°F/190°C. Butter 6 cups of a king-size muffin pan, then line with paper muffin liners.

2 Strip the flowers from the lavender and put into a processor with the superfine sugar. Blitz together.

3 Sift the flour into a large bowl.

4 In a pitcher, mix together the lemon zest and juice, eggs, sunflower oil, sour cream, and lavender sugar with a fork.

5 Pour the wet ingredients into the flour, then add scant ¹/₂ cup water and stir together to combine.

6 Spoon into the paper muffin liners and bake for 20–25 minutes, or until well risen and firm.

7 Cool in the pan for 5 minutes, then loosen with a palette knife and cool on a wire rack.

8 Sift the confectioners' sugar into a bowl and stir in enough lemon juice to make a smooth pouring consistency. Spoon over the muffins.

9 Top with a piece of fresh lavender to serve. Finish with candles.

Gooey chocolate Valentine's muffins

You can prepare these before you need them, then bake at the last minute to guarantee centers oozing with chocolate.

MAKES 12 / READY IN 40 MINUTES

6oz | 175g dark chocolate, broken into squares

¾ cup unsalted butter, cubed

4 eggs

4 egg yolks

scant ½ cup superfine sugar

½ cup all-purpose flour, sieved

2 tbsp confectioners' sugar, sifted

1 Heat the oven to 375°F/190°C. Line a 12-cup muffin pan with paper muffin liners.

2 Put the chocolate and butter in a heatproof bowl resting over a pan of simmering water and heat until melted. Stir once, then remove the bowl. Alternatively microwave on medium (500w) for 2 minutes, then stir and cook for another 2 minutes.

3 Whisk the whole eggs, yolks, and sugar with an electric mixer until very pale, foamy, and doubled in volume. Pour in the melted chocolate mixture and gently fold in, followed by the flour. Pour into the paper liners.

4 Bake for 7 minutes, or until firm on the outside and squidgy in the center.

5 To decorate, dust with confectioners' sugar or cut out some small heart shapes from card. Lay these on top of the muffins, then sprinkle with sifted confectioners' sugar. Carefully lift off the card hearts and serve.

Cook's tip: To prepare in advance, follow the recipe up to the end of step 3, then chill in the refrigerator for up to 5 hours. Then bake from chilled for 8 minutes .

Simnel muffins with marzipan

A spiced fruit cake with a surprise layer of marzipan, this was traditionally made to test a girl's skills as a cook. In Britain, Mothering Sunday falls in March, and girls who worked in domestic service were given the day off to bake a homemade simnel cake as a gift for their mother. If the cake remained moist and tasty until Easter Sunday, the girl was regarded as a good cook.

MAKES 12 / READY IN 40 MINUTES

1 tsp butter
1½ cups all-purpose flour, sifted
2 tsp baking powder
1 tsp ground nutmeg
1 tsp ground cinnamon
1 tsp ground allspice
scant ½ cup superfine sugar
generous ⅓ cup dark brown sugar
9oz | 250g luxury mixed dried fruit
finely grated zest and juice of 1 lemon
¾ cup butter, melted
3 eggs, lightly beaten
⅔ cup skim milk
12oz | 350g natural almond marzipan
6 tbsp apricot glaze

1 Heat the oven to 350°F/180°C. Butter a 12-cup large muffin pan.

2 Sift the flour, baking powder, nutmeg, cinnamon, and allspice into a large bowl. Stir in the sugars and dried fruit.

3 Add the lemon zest and juice, melted butter, eggs, and milk. Mix together until well combined.

4 Take half the marzipan and cut into 12 pieces. Roll each piece into a ball and flatten.

5 Put a generous spoonful of the simnel muffin mixture in each muffin cup. Top with a round of marzipan, then spoon on the rest of the muffin mixture.

6 Bake for 20 minutes. or until the cakes are risen, firm, pale golden, and a toothpick inserted into the center comes out clean.

7 Loosen the simnel muffins from the pan with a palette knife and cool on a wire rack.

8 Roll out the remaining marzipan and use a fluted 2in | 5cm cutter to cut out 12 flowers.

9 Brush the top of the muffins with apricot glaze and arrange the marzipan flowers on top. Flash under a hot broiler to brown the marzipan or blitz with a hot gun (brazier) to caramelize it.

Halloween pumpkin toffee cakes

Just the thing to serve up before or after Halloween—something tasty to make out of the scooped-out flesh from pumpkins. The recipe works equally well with hard squash like butternut if you want to make them throughout the year.

MAKES 12 / READY IN 50 MINUTES

1lb 2oz | 500g pumpkin flesh

1 cup sunflower oil

1½ cups dark brown sugar

3 large eggs

1½ cups self-rising flour

1 tsp baking soda

1 tsp each ground ginger, cinnamon, and allspice

12oz | 350g jar Dulce de Leche (banoffee sauce, found alongside ice cream toppings in the supermarket)

12 ready-to-eat dried apricots

Cook's tip: Instead of fresh pumpkin, you could use a 1lb | 450g can of cooked puréed pumpkin to save time.

1 Preheat the oven to 350°F/180°C. Line a 12-cup muffin pan with paper muffin liners.

2 Put the pumpkin flesh into a heatproof bowl with 1 tbsp water. Microwave on high (850w) for 8 minutes. Or boil in a pan for 15 minutes, then drain.

3 Blend until smooth with a hand blender.

4 Put the oil, sugar, and eggs in a large bowl and whisk together using a hand-held electric mixer until thick and pale.

5 Stir in the flour, baking soda, ginger, cinnamon, and allspice. Add the pumpkin purée.

6 Spoon the mixture into the paper liners and bake for 20 minutes.

7 Cool in the pan for 10 minutes, then transfer to a wire rack to cool.

8 Spread a spoonful of the Dulce de Leche over the top of each cooled cake and top with a dried apricot.

Vanilla surprise christening cakes

These will be well received whether you're serving them up in the morning with coffee or in the afternoon for tea. The child-friendly flavors of vanilla with a surprise banana center make an interesting alternative to a classic fruit cake. Banana chips are my chosen easiest decoration. However, if you're the creative type, you could pipe cute pastel-colored icing decorations such as a bottle, silver spoon, or the baby's initials.

MAKES 12 / READY IN 50 MINUTES

1⅔ cups all-purpose flour

1 tbsp baking powder

½ tsp baking soda

generous ¾ cup buttermilk

2 tsp vanilla extract

½ cup butter, melted

1 cup superfine sugar

3 large eggs

2 bananas, mashed with 1 tsp lemon juice

For the frosting:

½ cup lowfat cream cheese

scant ½ cup butter, at room temperature

drop of vanilla extract

1 cup unrefined confectioners' sugar

12 chewy banana chips

1 Heat the oven to 350°F/180°C. Line a 12-cup muffin tray with paper liners.

2 Sift the flour, baking powder, and baking soda into a large bowl.

3 In a pitcher mix the buttermilk, vanilla extract, butter, sugar, and eggs with a fork.

4 Pour the wet ingredients into the dry.

5 Half-fill the paper liners with muffin mixture and top with a spoonful of mashed banana. Top with the rest of the muffin mixture and bake for 20 minutes, or until muffins are risen and firm and a toothpick inserted into the center comes out clean.

6 For the frosting, beat together the cream cheese, butter, and vanilla to combine. Sift in the confectioners' sugar and mix together.

7 Spread the frosting onto the cooled muffins with a palette knife. Top each one with a banana chip or your chosen decoration.

Christmas spice muffins with brandy butter frosting

I first made these one Christmas Eve. Friends were coming for tea and I realized at 3pm that I'd failed to make a traditional Christmas cake. The result: these mini cakes, lighter than the overfruity, sometimes dry, seasonal cake. They're sure to become a new family tradition.

1 Put the dried fruit into a sealable container or large jar. Pour over the alcohol, reserving 1 tbsp and heat in the microwave on high (850w) for 2 minutes to help plump up the fruit. Alternatively, put the fruit and alcohol into a pan and heat gently for 5 minutes.

2 Heat the oven to 325°F/170°C. Line 15 cups in two muffin pans with paper muffin liners.

3 Pour half the mixture into a food processor and blend until smooth.

4 Put the flour, baking powder, allspice, ginger, and sugar into a large bowl. Add the butter and eggs and stir together to combine.

5 Stir in the puréed fruit and the remaining soaked fruit and alcohol to combine evenly.

6 Spoon the mixture into the muffin liners and bake for 30 minutes, or until risen, firm, and a toothpick inserted into the center comes out clean.

7 Pierce the muffins in several places with a toothpick and drizzle over the remaining alcohol. Cool and store in an airtight container for up to one week.

8 To make the brandy butter frosting, put the butter and confectioners' sugar into a food processor and blend until smooth. Add the cream cheese and alcohol and stir until combined. Chill until ready to serve the muffins.

9 Use a palette knife to spread the frosting over the muffins, then sprinkle each one with silver balls to decorate. Once topped, keep in the refrigerator for up to 1 week.

Cook's tip: The longer you let the dried fruit and alcohol soak, the more intense the flavor will be. Even an hour's soaking is a plus, but letting it macerate for up to a month makes the flavor really impressive!

MAKES 15 / READY IN 1 HOUR

11oz | 300g mixed dried fruit

1¼ cups dark rum, sherry, brandy, or Southern Comfort

1⅔ cups self-rising flour

½ tsp baking powder

4 tbsp ground allspice

1 tsp ground ginger

scant 1¼ cups dark brown sugar

generous 2 cups butter, softened

4 eggs, lightly beaten

For the brandy butter frosting:

generous ½ cup unsalted butter, melted

1½ cups confectioners' sugar

⅔ cup cream cheese

1 tbsp dark rum, sherry, brandy, or Southern Comfort

about 45 edible silver balls

White chocolate rose wedding muffins

There is no need to save these just for weddings. They taste great without the topping too.

MAKES 6 KING-SIZE MUFFINS, OR 12 REGULAR MUFFINS / READY IN 50 MINUTES

1 Heat the oven to 400°F/200°C. Line a 6-cup king-size muffin pan with paper muffin liners (or line a 12-cup regular muffin pan with paper muffin liners).

2 Sift both flours, the baking powder, and the baking soda into a large bowl. Add the sugar, orange zest and juice, and white chocolate and mix together.

3 In a pitcher mix together the melted butter, eggs, milk, and vanilla extract.

4 Pour the wet ingredients onto the dry ingredients and stir together to combine.

5 Spoon the mixture into the prepared pans and bake for 25 minutes. (Regular muffins should be baked for 15 minutes.)

6 Loosen muffins with a palette knife and cool on a wire rack. Pierce several times with a toothpick and pour over the sweet wine.

7 Put the chocolate and corn syrup into a heatproof bowl, resting over a pan of simmering water. Heat for a few minutes until melted. Remove from the heat and sift in the confectioners' sugar and stir together to form into a ball.

8 Cut the white chocolate icing into 6 pieces and mold each piece into a rose. Position on top of muffins to decorate.

generous ¾ cup all-purpose flour
1⅔ cups self-rising flour
1 tsp baking powder
½ tsp baking soda
1 cup superfine sugar
grated zest and juice of 1 orange
3½oz | 100g white chocolate, chopped
scant 1 cup butter, melted
2 large eggs
generous ¾ cup skim milk
1 tsp vanilla extract
⅔ cup sweet dessert wine

For the topping:
7oz | 200g white chocolate, chopped
5oz | 150g corn syrup
1 cup unrefined confectioners' sugar

Amaretto and sugared almond muffins

Just want to say congratulations to celebrate a special occasion? These muffins fit the bill perfectly. Sugared almonds make a classy decoration and are available in a multitude of colors, from subtle pastels to glitzy metallics, so you're bound to find something to suit. These are also good for weddings.

MAKES 6 KING-SIZE MUFFINS / READY IN 40 MINUTES

1 Heat the oven to 375°F/190°C. Butter a 6-cup king-size muffin pan and line with paper muffin liners.

2 Sift the flour and baking soda into a large bowl, then stir in the ground almonds, sugar, unbeaten egg whites, milk, and softened butter. Stir to combine.

3 Spoon the mixture into the paper muffin liners and bake for 20 minutes, or until well risen and firm.

4 Drizzle each muffin with the amaretto liqueur.

5 Sift the confectioners' sugar into a bowl and stir in the water and almond extract to make a smooth icing. Spoon the icing over each muffin. Top with a sugared almond to decorate.

1 tsp butter
generous ¾ cup self-rising flour
½ tsp baking soda
1¼ cups ground almonds
generous ½ cup superfine sugar
3 egg whites
⅔ cup skim milk
½ cup butter, softened
3 tbsp Amaretto liqueur

For the topping:
1¾ cups confectioners' sugar
2 tbsp water
½ tsp almond extract
6 sugared almonds

Devil's food birthday muffins

Little chocolate cakes that are light enough to enjoy as a birthday treat and gooey enough to feel indulgent.

1 Pour the milk into a pitcher and squeeze in the lemon juice. Stir and let stand for a few minutes to sour. Heat the oven to 375°F/190°C and line two 12-cup regular muffin pans with 20 paper liners.

2 Put the butter and half the sugar into a large bowl and use an electric mixer to cream together until pale, light, and fluffy.

3 Add the rest of the sugar, then gradually whisk in the eggs.

4 Sift half of the flour, baking soda, baking powder, and cocoa onto the mixture and pour over half the soured milk. Whisk together, then whisk in the rest of the flour and milk.

5 Spoon the mixture into the prepared muffin pans and bake for 20 minute, or until they are well risen, firm yet springy, and a toothpick inserted into the center comes out clean.

6 Pierce the muffins several times with a toothpick and drizzle a little Southern Comfort onto each one, if using.

7 For the topping, put the sugar, cream of tartar, and egg whites into a large heatproof bowl over a pan of simmering water. Use a hand-held electric whisk to whisk continuously until the mixture is glossy, holds its shape, and looks like meringue. This will take 3–4 minutes.

8 Spread the frosting over the top of the cakes with a palette knife. Drag a vegetable peeler over the chocolate to make curls and sprinkle over the top of the cakes.

Cook's tip: To make a personalized chocolate decoration, break up the chocolate and microwave in a bowl on medium (500w) for 2 minutes until just softened. Spoon the melted chocolate into a paper pastry bag. Line a tray with parchment paper. Snip off the end of the pastry bag and gently squeeze the chocolate onto the parchment-lined tray into your chosen shape. Chill for at least 1 hour. Carefully ease a palette knife between the chocolate and the paper to release and position on top of each cake.

MAKES 20 REGULAR MUFFINS / READY IN 1 HOUR

generous 1½ cups skim milk

juice of ½ a lemon

¾ cup unsalted butter, at room temperature

scant 2 cups superfine sugar

3 eggs

2⅔ cups all-purpose flour

1 tsp baking soda

2 tsp baking powder

4 tbsp unsweetened cocoa

3 tbsp Southern Comfort, optional

For the frosting:

1¾ cups superfine sugar

½ tsp cream of tartar

2 egg whites

3½oz | 100g dark chocolate, to decorate

Anniversary pistachio and rose water muffins

An intriguing recipe with a delicate flavor. Why not serve these on a large plate or tray made from the material traditionally associated with each year's celebration?

MAKES 12 REGULAR MUFFINS / READY IN 35 MINUTES

1½ cups all-purpose flour

1 tbsp baking powder

generous ½ cup superfine sugar

⅔ cup pistachios, coarsely chopped in a food processor

scant ½ cup butter, melted

⅔ cup sour cream

⅓ cup honey

2 eggs

For the rose water icing:

2 cups white confectioners' sugar

1 tsp culinary rose water

3 tbsp boiling water

candied rose petals, to decorate

1 Heat the oven to 375°F/190°C. Line a 12-cup muffin pan with paper muffin liners.

2 Sift the flour and baking powder into a bowl and stir in the sugar and pistachios.

3 In a pitcher mix the melted butter, sour cream, runny honey, and eggs with a fork.

4 Pour the wet ingredients onto the dry and stir together until just smooth.

5 Pour the mixture equally into the muffin liners and bake for 20 minutes, or until risen, firm and springy, and a toothpick inserted into the center comes out clean.

6 Sift the confectioners' sugar into a bowl, then add the rose water and 2 tbsp of boiling water. Mix together until it is the consistency of single cream. Add a little more water if needed.

7 Spoon the rose water icing on top of the muffins. Let set, then sprinkle over a few rose petals to serve.

Internationally Inspired

The interesting thing about baking is that although everyone loves tucking into warm, homemade goodies worldwide, cooks' methods vary greatly from one country to the next. My starting point for any recipe tends to be whatever's quickest and easiest, which is why I love traditional American muffins. However, for an authentic continental flavor a little extra effort may be required. This chapter features ten of my favorite recipes from all corners of the globe, several of them using classic techniques that many purists could dispute make them worthy of being called a muffin. But I reckon if they're cooked in a muffin pan they have every right to be included.

American cranberry and orange muffins

The tanginess of cranberries gives a refreshing taste to these muffins, and is complemented by the orange zest.

MAKES 6 KING-SIZE MUFFINS / READY IN 30 MINUTES

scant 1 cup fresh or frozen cranberries
¼ cup confectioners' sugar
1⅔ cups all-purpose flour
2 tsp baking powder
¾ cup superfine sugar
finely grated zest of 1 large orange
1 large egg
1 cup milk
¼ cup unsalted butter, melted
confectioners' sugar, sifted for dusting

1 Heat the oven to 400°F/200°C. Line a 6-cup king-size muffin pan with paper muffin liners.
2 Toss the cranberries in the confectioners' sugar to coat.
3 Sift the flour and baking powder into a large bowl. Stir in the sugar, orange zest, and cranberries.
4 In a large pitcher mix together the egg, milk, and butter. Add the wet ingredients to the dry ingredients and gently stir everything together until just combined.
5 Spoon into the muffin liners and bake for 15–20 minutes, or until well risen and firm.
6 Cool on a wire rack and dust with confectioners' sugar to serve.

Cook's tip: Cranberries are available for only a short season, so stock up whilst they're in the shops and freeze for up to 6 months. Alternatively, use scant ⅔ cup of dried cranberries, which are available all year. Omit the confectioners' sugar.

American blueberry and sour cream muffins

Blueberries may sometimes be pricey but they're worth it. They're considered a superfood, as they're so high in vitamin C. But don't give yourself a false sense of security—it's no excuse for gorging on these delicious muffins, as they do also contain butter and sugar; a sprinkling of fresh blueberries over plain yogurt with a handful of oats would be healthier!

MAKES 6 KING-SIZE MUFFINS / READY IN 30 MINUTES

1⅓ cups all-purpose flour
½ tsp baking soda
2 tsp baking powder
½ cup superfine sugar
pinch of salt
6 tbsp butter, melted
generous ¾ cup sour cream
1 large egg
1⅓ cups blueberries

1 Heat the oven to 400°F/200°C. Line a 6-cup king-size muffin pan with paper liners.
2 Sift the flour, baking soda, and baking powder into a bowl. Add the sugar and salt.
3 Pour the butter, sour cream, and egg into a pitcher and mix together with a fork.
4 Pour the wet ingredients into the dry ingredients and add the blueberries. Gently stir everything together until just mixed.
5 Spoon the mixture into the muffin liners and bake for 15–20 minutes, or until they are well risen and firm.

French madeleines

These are tiny little buns that keep really well. The mix here actually improves if it's made ahead of time and chilled before baking.

1 Brush 18 cups in regular muffin pans with 2 tbsp of the melted butter and let stand for a few minutes, then dust with flour.

2 Whisk the eggs, sugar, and lemon zest in a bowl with an electric whisk until they are pale, creamy, and thick enough to leave a trail when the beaters are lifted.

3 Sift in half the flour with the baking powder and salt. Carefully pour half the melted butter around the sides of the bowl and gently fold in. Repeat with the remaining butter and flour and gently fold in. Cover and chill for 45 minutes. (This gives madeleines their characteristic dense texture.)

4 Heat the oven to 425°F/220°C. Pour the mixture into the prepared pans.

5 Bake the madeleines for 10 minutes, or until well risen and golden. Ease out of the pans with a palette knife and cool on a wire rack. Dust with confectioners' sugar.

MAKES 18 SMALL CUPCAKE- SIZED MUFFINS / READY IN 1 HOUR

scant ⅔ cup unsalted butter, melted

all-purpose flour, for dusting

4 eggs

generous ½ cup superfine sugar

finely grated zest of 1 lemon

generous ¾ cup plain white flour

1 tsp baking powder

pinch of salt

2 tbsp confectioners' sugar, for dusting

Greek lemon syrup cakes

Here's semolina in a whole new guise—added to flour with almonds to add a scrumptious mealy texture to a dessert muffin. Drenched in fragrant cardamom and orange flower syrup, these are really special.

1 Heat the oven to 400°F/200°C. Grease 8 king-size muffin cups (two pans) with butter.

2 Put the butter and sugar into the bowl of a food processor and whiz together until pale, light, and fluffy.

3 Add the lemon zest and juice, eggs, semolina, baking powder, and ground almonds and whiz until smooth.

4 Spoon the mixture into the prepared pans and bake for 15 minutes, or until just firm. Let stand in the pans for 5 minutes, then loosen with a palette knife and put the cakes onto a shallow tray to cool.

5 To make the syrup, put the orange shreds into a pan and add the orange juice. Add the cardamom pods, cinnamon stick, sugar, water, and lemon juice.

6 Heat gently to dissolve the sugar, then boil rapidly for 3–5 minutes, or until syrupy. Remove from the heat and add the orange flower water.

7 Pour the syrup over the cakes to drench them, leaving excess in the tray. Cool, then cover and chill. Serve drizzled with extra syrup and a dollop of Greek-style yogurt.

MAKES 8 KING-SIZE MUFFINS / READY IN 35 MINUTES

½ cup unsalted butter, softened, plus extra for greasing

½ cup superfine sugar

finely grated zest and juice of 2 lemons

2 eggs

scant ⅔ cup semolina

2 tsp baking powder

generous 1 cup ground almonds

For the syrup:

juice and peel of 1 orange, removed with a vegetable peeler and cut into needle shreds

8 cardamom pods, crushed

1 cinnamon stick, broken into pieces

1½ cups superfine sugar

generous ¾ cup water

juice of ½ lemon

2 tbsp orange flower water

Turkish coffee and nut muffins

Really strong, freshly made espresso coffee gives these muffins an authentic flavor, although you could use 2 tbsp of instant espresso powder if you're not a fresh coffee fiend.

1 Heat the oven to 350°F/180°C. Line a 12-cup muffin pan with 8 paper muffin liners.

2 Sift the flour into a bowl with the baking powder. Add the toasted ground hazelnuts and sugar.

3 In a large pitcher mix together the melted butter, coffee liquid, and eggs with a fork.

4 Pour the wet ingredients into the dry and stir together until well combined.

5 Spoon into the paper muffin liners and sprinkle over the chopped hazelnuts.

6 Bake for 20 minutes, or until well risen and firm.

MAKES 8 REGULAR MUFFINS / READY IN 30 MINUTES

scant 1¼ cups all-purpose flour

2 tsp baking powder

scant ¼ cup toasted hazelnuts, blended until ground

scant 1 cup dark brown sugar

scant ½ cup butter, melted

6 tbsp very strong espresso coffee

3 eggs

scant ¼ cup toasted hazelnuts, chopped

Italian pine nut and almond muffins

You may already use pine nuts to make pesto or in salads, but they're also gorgeous in sweet dishes. The light olive oil works really well in this, too.

1 Heat the oven to 350°F/180°C. Grease a 12-cup muffin pan.

2 Sift the flour and baking powder into a large bowl. Stir in the ground pine nuts, ground almonds, superfine sugar, and lemon zest.

3 Pour the sour cream into a pitcher and add the eggs and olive oil. Mix together with a fork.

4 Gently stir the wet ingredients to the dry to combine.

5 Spoon the muffin mixture into the greased muffin cups. Sprinkle over the pine nuts and chopped almonds.

6 Bake for 12 minutes, or until a toothpick inserted into the center comes out clean.

7 Cool on a wire rack and dust with sifted confectioners' sugar to finish.

MAKES 12 REGULAR MUFFINS / READY IN 30 MINUTES

1 tsp butter, to grease

scant 1¼ cups all-purpose flour

2 tsp baking powder

⅓ cup pine nuts, blended in a processor until ground

generous ½ cup ground almonds

generous ½ cup superfine sugar

finely grated zest of 1 small lemon

1 cup sour cream

2 eggs

5 tbsp light olive oil

scant ¼ cup pine nuts

scant ¼ cup whole almonds, chopped

2 tbsp confectioners' sugar, to dust

French tarte tatin

Enjoy this warm as a perfect dessert or treat with a coffee.

MAKES 6 REGULAR MUFFINS / READY IN 1 HOUR

1 For the topping, melt the butter over a low heat in a frying pan, then add the ½ cup sugar and heat until melted.

2 Add the apples, then cover and let stand for 5 minutes without turning. Gently stir and cook for an additional 5 minutes, or until the sugar has caramelized to a rich golden brown.

3 Heat the oven to 350°F/180°C. Line a 6-cup muffin pan with paper muffin liners.

4 For the base, sift the flour and baking powder into a bowl. Add the sugar and stir to combine.

5 Put the sour cream, eggs, butter, water, and vanilla extract into a pitcher and stir together using a fork.

6 Pour the wet ingredients onto the dry and stir gently to combine.

7 Arrange the caramelized apple slices in the base of each muffin liner. Spoon over the muffin mixture and bake for 20 minutes, or until the muffins are well risen and springy.

8 Upturn muffins onto serving plate and peel away the paper muffin liners.

For the topping:

¼ cup butter

½ cup superfine sugar

1lb 11oz | 750g eating apples, peeled, quartered, cored, and sliced, and tossed in 2 tbsp lemon juice

For the base:

1½ cups all-purpose flour

2 tsp baking powder

scant 1 cup superfine sugar

generous 1 cup sour cream

2 eggs

6 tbsp butter, melted

scant ½ cup water

1 tsp vanilla extract

Jamaican Bun

My family adores this. We first discovered it sold as large sweet bread loaves in West Indian bakeries. A kind midwife revealed the recipe for a homemade version while I was in labor with my third child! In the mêlée I lost that original recipe but have since devised this one myself. Traditionally served at Easter time, but great anytime served with slices of cheddar cheese.

MAKES 12 REGULAR MUFFINS / READY IN 1 HOUR

1 Heat the oven to 375°F/190°C. Grease a 12-cup muffin pan with butter

2 Sift the flour, baking soda, allspice, and nutmeg into a large bowl. Add the sugar and golden raisins.

3 Pour in the butter, eggs, stout, milk, and lemon juice and stir well together to make a soft dropping consistency.

4 Spoon the mixture into the buttered muffin pan and bake for 40 minutes, or until a toothpick inserted into the center comes out clean.

1 tsp butter, to grease

1⅔ cups self-rising flour

½ tsp baking soda

1 tsp ground allspice

½ tsp ground nutmeg

1 cup dark brown sugar

scant 1 cup golden raisins

½ cup butter, melted

2 eggs, lightly beaten

scant ½ cup stout

scant ½ cup milk

1 tbsp lemon juice

Spanish orange and almond muffins

You may take one look at this and flinch at the thought of boiling and blending an orange at the beginning of this recipe. I urge you to give it a try and I think you'll agree that the extra effort is rewarded by the moist texture of the finished muffin and improved even more when they're drenched in orange syrup.

MAKES 12 REGULAR MUFFINS / READY INN 1 HOUR

2 unwaxed oranges, washed

1⅓ cups ground almonds

scant 1 cup superfine sugar

2 tsp baking powder

6 tbsp butter, melted, plus extra for greasing

4 eggs

For the orange syrup:

generous 1 cup superfine sugar

⅔ cup orange juice

scant ½ cup water

1 Pierce the oranges several times with a sharp knife and put into a heatproof bowl. Cover with boiling water. Microwave on high (850w) for 20 minutes, or until the orange is really tender. Alternatively, put the oranges into a pan, then cover with boiling water and simmer for 1 hour, or until tender.

2 Put the whole drained oranges into a food processor and blend together until they turn into a smooth purée.

3 Heat the oven to 170°C/325°F/gas 3. Grease a 12-cup muffin pan.

4 Put the almonds, sugar, and baking powder into a bowl. Pour in the melted butter, puréed oranges, and eggs and mix together thoroughly.

5 Spoon into the prepared pans and bake for 40 minutes, or until a toothpick inserted into the center comes out clean.

6 For the syrup, put the sugar, orange juice, and water into a pan. Boil for 15 minutes until the liquid turns syrupy.

7 Loosen the warm cakes with a palette knife and put onto serving plates. Pour over the syrup to serve. Lovely served with a generous dollop of sour cream.

Canadian maple syrup and pecan

I was once was lucky enough to see sap-collecting from a maple tree in snowy North America. This liquid is boiled so that the water evaporates but the sugar stays, leaving a divinely sticky syrup. This is a wonderful natural sweet product that deserves respect.

MAKES 12 REGULAR MUFFINS / READY IN 35 MINUTES

1½ cups all-purpose flour

2 tsp baking powder

½ cup dark brown sugar

1 cup pecans, coarsely chopped

scant ½ cup butter, melted

generous ½ cup maple syrup

2 eggs

4 tbsp maple syrup, to glaze

1 Heat the oven to 375°F/190°C. Line a 12-cup muffin pan with paper muffin liners.

2 Sift the flour and baking powder into a bowl and stir in the sugar and pecans.

3 Mix the melted butter, maple syrup, and eggs in a pitcher with a fork.

4 Pour the wet ingredients onto the dry and stir together until just smooth.

5 Pour the mixture into the muffin liners and bake for 20 minutes, or until risen, firm and springy, and a toothpick inserted into the center comes out clean.

6 Brush the warm muffins with maple syrup.

Nutritional Values (per serving)

KEY

All values are per muffin

Figures in ( ) indicate the number of muffins each recipe makes

Tr indicates that a small trace of the nutrient is present

Recipe	Energy (cal)	Fat (g)	Saturated Fats (g)	Carbs (g)	Fiber (g)	Vegetarian (•)
Brilliant for Breakfast						
Whole-grain honey muffins (9)	182	9	1	22	2	•
Four-seed muffins (12)	188	9	1	29	6	•
Apricot and oat muffins (12)	250	9	1	39	3	•
Whole-wheat apple (12)	200	8	1	29	2	•
English muffins (8)	250	6	3	45	2	•
English muffins (10)	200	5	3	36	1	•
Bacon, cheese, and maple syrup (8)	164	7	3	20	1	
Muesli muffins (9)	240	12	2	32	2	•
Smoked salmon and chive (9)	190	10	2	20	1	
Smoked salmon and chive (24)	176	8	2	20	1	
Marmalade orange muffins (12)	200	8	1	31	2	•
Bran and banana muffins (12)	170	7	1	25	3	•
Children's Choice						
Chocolate chip muffins (12)	160	9	3	19	Tr	•
Crunchy peanut butter muffins (24)	94	6	1	10	1	•
Banana and honey muffins (24)	60	3	Tr	8	Tr	•
Chocolate muffins (17)	180	8	4	25	Tr	•
Coconut muffins (24)	90	4	2	12	1	•
Lemon curd muffins (12)	190	7	1	33	1	•
Pink fairy muffins (12)	160	5	1	29	Tr	•
Marbled soccer muffins (12)	190	9	3	24	Tr	•
Jelly surprise muffins (12)	147	6	1	24	1	•
Squashed fly muffins (12)	140	5	1	21	Tr	•
Classic Combinations						
Lemon and poppy seed muffins (12)	240	12	2	30	1	•
Sticky ginger and corn syrup muffins (12)	200	9	1	29	1	•
Buttery vanilla muffins (12)	270	11	7	41	1	•

Recipe	Energy (cal)	Fat (g)	Saturated Fats (g)	Carbs (g)	Fiber (g)	Vegetarian (•)
Apple and cinnamon crumble muffins (12)	170	6	1	28	1	•
Mincemeat and rum muffins (12)	250	6	3	46	1	•
Cheese and chutney muffins (12)	200	9	6	23	1	•
Cappuccino and chocolate chip (12)	280	13	8	40	1	•
Banana and toffee muffins (12)	220	7	4	39	1	•
Carrot and cream cheese muffins (8)	536	32	13	59	1	•
Chocolate brownie muffins (12)	390	22	13	45	Tr	•
Something Savory						
Spicy tex-mex muffins (12)	240	22	6	6	Tr	•
Walnut, leek, and bacon muffins (12)	220	20	9	6	1	
Mushroom and sunblush tomato muffins (12)	170	8	2	20	1	•
Sweet pepper and mozzarella cheese muffins (9)	230	10	3	29	2	•
Italian pizza muffins (12)	200	11	4	18	1	
Polenta and cheese muffins (9)	170	4	2	27	1	•
Feta and olive muffins (12)	220	13	4	20	1	•
Pesto muffins (9)	280	18	4	20	1	•
Shrimp and peppadew muffins (12)	200	13	5	17	1	
Cheese, sage, and onion muffins (12)	170	10	3	16	1	•
Healthy Selection						
Blueberry and oat muffins (8)	260	7	1	45	3	•
Lowfat berry and apple muffins (12)	112	1	Tr	24	6	•
Lowfat yogurt and sour cherry (12)	130	Tr	Tr	30	1	•
Ricotta and spinach (12)	160	14	7	2	Tr	•
Cinnamon English muffins (10)	200	5	3	37	1	•
Whole-wheat yogurt and malted raisin (12)	130	Tr	Tr	30	1	•
Butter-free chocolate and prune (11)	213	6	1	49	2	•
Tangy cranberry (12)	180	5	3	34	1	•

Recipe	Energy (cal)	Fat (g)	Saturated Fats (g)	Carbs (g)	Fiber (g)	Vegetarian (•)
Egg and bacon treats (9)	210	17	9	1	0	
Lowfat golden raisin and bran English muffins (10)	200	3	2	38	5	•
Special Diets						
Cornmeal scones (9)	190	6	3	29	1	•
Carrot and pineapple muffins (12)	270	13	2	38	1	•
Buckwheat and apple muffins (12)	240	6	1	44	2	•
Gooseberry and almond muffins (12)	300	17	2	33	3	•
Sweet potato muffins (9)	280	2	2	41	1	•
Bran, date, and prune muffins (12)	210	8	1	30	3	•
Oatmeal and raspberry muffins (12)	200	5	1	37	1	•
Lactose-free zucchini muffins (12)	310	15	2	44	1	•
Herb popovers (6)	150	4	1	21	1	•
Sugar-free double-corn muffins (9)	200	9	1	25	1	•
Scones						
English afternoon tea scones (8)	280	13	8	40	1	•
Malt grain scones (8)	150	6	3	23	2	•
Sunflower seed and honey scones (8)	230	12	6	27	2	•
Cheddar and thyme scones (8)	170	8	5	22	1	•
Carrot and raisin scones (8)	210	6	4	37	1	•
Whole-wheat scone round (6)	220	8	5	35	3	•
Vanilla and buttermilk scones (8)	200	6	4	32	1	•
Buttermilk drop scones (6)	220	8	3	32	1	•
Blueberry cinnamon scones (8)	220	6	4	37	1	•
Cranberry and walnut scones (8)	250	10	4	37	2	•
Time to Indulge						
Preserved ginger muffins (6)	353	15	9	50	7	•
Strawberries and cream (6)	562	27	11	76	2	•
Mixed nut muffins (4)	677	37	3	81	5	•
Coconut, carrot, pecan, and pineapple muffins (6)	734	40	11	90	5	•
Sticky toffee and date muffins (8)	503	23	14	75	2	•
Vanilla bean muffins (6)	400	17	10	59	1	•

Recipe	Energy (cal)	Fat (g)	Saturated Fats (g)	Carbs (g)	Fiber (g)	Vegetarian (•)
Dark chocolate truffle muffins (12)	520	30	18	56	1	•
Tiramisu muffins (12)	420	23	10	50	1	•
Luxury lemon muffins (8)	405	12	7	71	1	•
Mini golden Victoria sandwiches (12)	373	21	13	43	1	•
Fit for a Celebration						
Lavender and lemon birthday muffins (6)	534	28	7	69	1	•
Gooey chocolate Valentine's muffins (12)	280	20	12	20	Tr	•
Simnel muffins with marzipan (12)	436	18	8	67	2	•
Halloween Pumpkin toffee cakes (12)	450	22	3	60	1	•
Vanilla surprise christening cakes (12)	410	21	13	53	1	•
Christmas spice muffins with brandy butter frosting (15)	530	29	18	55	1	•
White chocolate rose wedding muffins (6)	1065	46	27	153	2	•
White chocolate rose wedding muffins (12)	533	23	14	77	1	•
Amaretto and sugared almond muffins (6)	585	29	12	73	2	•
Devil's food birthday muffins (20)	320	10	6	56	1	•
Anniversary pistachio and rose water muffins (12)	350	13	5	57	1	•
Internationally Inspired						
American cranberry and orange muffins (6)	352	9	5	66	2	•
American blueberry and sour cream muffins (6)	376	19	11	45	2	•
French madeleines (18)	120	8	5	8	Tr	•
Greek lemon syrup cakes (8)	470	22	10	65	1	•
Turkish coffee and nut muffins (8)	310	15	8	40	1	•
Italian pine nut and almond muffins (12)	290	19	5	26	1	•
French tarte tatin (6)	690	36	23	90	1	•
Jamaican bun (12)	240	10	6	34	1	•
Spanish orange and almond muffins (12)	280	13	4	38	2	•
Canadian maple syrup and pecan (12)	300	15	5	38	1	•

Index

Recipes are for American muffins unless otherwise indicated. Page numbers in **bold** denote illustrations.